The Talking Machine Industry

THE TALKING MACHINE INDUSTRY

PITMAN'S
COMMON COMMODITIES
AND INDUSTRIES SERIES

Each book in crown 8vo, illustrated, 3/- net

TEA. By A. Ibbetson
COFFEE. By B. B. Keable
SUGAR. By Geo. Martineau
OILS. By C. Ainsworth Mitchell
WHEAT. By Andrew Millar
RUBBER. By C. Beadle and H. P. Stevens
IRON AND STEEL. By C. Hood
COPPER. By H. K. Picard
COAL. By F. H. Wilson
TIMBER. By W. Bullock
COTTON. By R. J. Peake
SILK. By Luther Hooper
WOOL. By J. A. Hunter
LINEN. By Alfred S. Moore
TOBACCO. By A. E. Tanner
LEATHER. By K. J. Adcock
KNITTED FABRICS. By J. Chamberlain and J. H. Quilter
CLAYS. By Alfred B. Searle
PAPER. By Harry A. Maddox
SOAP By W. A. Simmons
THE MOTOR INDUSTRY. By Horace Wyatt
GLASS. By Percival Marson
GUMS AND RESINS. By E. J. Parry
THE BOOT AND SHOE INDUSTRY. By J. S. Harding
GAS. By W. H. Y. Webber
FURNITURE. By H. E. Binstead
COAL TAR. By A. R. Warnes
PETROLEUM. By A. Lidgett
SALT. By A. F. Calvert
ZINC. By T. E. Lones
PHOTOGRAPHY. By Wm. Gamble
ASBESTOS. By A. L. Summers
SILVER. By Benjamin White
CARPETS. By Reginald S. Brinton
PAINTS AND VARNISHES. By A. S. Jennings
CORDAGE AND CORDAGE HEMP. By T. Woodhouse and P. Kilgour
ACIDS AND ALKALIS. By G. H. J. Adlam
ELECTRICITY. By R. E. Neale
ALUMINIUM. By G. Mortimer
GOLD. By Benjamin White
BUTTER AND CHEESE. By C. W. Walker-Tisdale and Jean Jones
THE BRITISH CORN TRADE. By A. Barker
LEAD. By J. A. Smythe
ENGRAVING. By T. W. Lascelles
STONES AND QUARRIES. By J. Allen Howe

EXPLOSIVES. By S. I. Levy
THE CLOTHING INDUSTRY. By B. W. Poole
TELEGRAPHY, TELEPHONY, AND WIRELESS. By J. Poole
PERFUMERY. By E. J. Parry
THE ELECTRIC LAMP INDUSTRY. By G. Arncliffe Percival
ICE AND COLD STORAGE. By B. H. Springett
GLOVES. By B. E. Ellis
JUTE. By T. Woodhouse and P. Kilgour
DRUGS IN COMMERCE. By J. Humphrey
THE FILM INDUSTRY. By Davidson Boughey
CYCLE INDUSTRY. By W. Grew
SULPHUR. By Harold A. Auden
TEXTILE BLEACHING. By Alec B. Steven
WINE. By Andre L. Simon
IRONFOUNDING. By B. Whiteley
COTTON SPINNING. By A. S. Wade
ALCOHOL. By C. Simmonds
CONCRETE AND REINFORCED CONCRETE. By W. N. Twelvetrees
SPONGES. By E. J. J. Cresswell
WALL PAPER. By G. Whiteley Ward
CLOCKS AND WATCHES. By G. L. Overton
ANTHRACITE. By A. L. Summers
INCANDESCENT LIGHTING. By S. I. Levy
THE FISHING INDUSTRY. By W. E. Gibbs
OIL FOR POWER PURPOSES. By S. H. North
STARCH. By H. A. Auden
TALKING MACHINES. By O. Mitchell
NICKEL. By B. H. White
PLAYER PIANO. By D. M. Wilson
INTERNAL COMBUSTION ENGINES. By J. Okill
DYES. By A. J. Hall
MOTOR BOATS. By F. Strickland
VELVET. By J. H. Cooke
THE STRAW HAT INDUSTRY. By H. Inwards
BRUSHES. By W. Kiddier
PATENT FUELS. By J. A. Greene and F. Mollwo Perkin
FURS. By J. C. Sachs

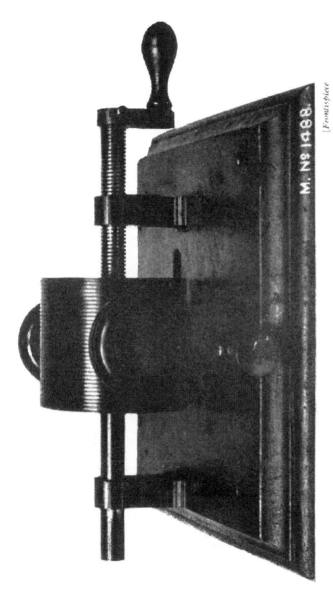

M. Nº 1488.

THE FIRST TALKING MACHINE IN THE WORLD, AS INVENTED BY THOMAS ALVA EDISON.

From a Photograph in the possession of *The Talking Machine News.*

(1466E)

PITMAN'S COMMON COMMODITIES
AND INDUSTRIES

THE
TALKING MACHINE
INDUSTRY

BY

OGILVIE MITCHELL

ASSOCIATE EDITOR AND REVIEWER
"TALKING MACHINE NEWS"

LONDON
SIR ISAAC PITMAN & SONS, LTD.
PARKER STREET, KINGSWAY, W.C.2
BATH, MELBOURNE, TORONTO, NEW YORK

PREFACE

IN writing this little book, I have endeavoured, as far as possible, to avoid all technicalities and abstruse phraseology. In short, my aim has been to make it "understanded of the people." For guidance, I have dipped liberally into my friend Mr. Henry Seymour's illuminating volume entitled *The Reproduction of Sound*, the most valuable work on the subject I know. Also, I have delved into Tyndall's *Lectures on Sound*, and have, of course, rummaged through the *Encyclopaedia Britannica*. Mainly, however, I have obtained my information from back numbers of *The Talking Machine News*, the oldest paper entirely devoted to the trade in the world. It is now entering upon the twentieth year of its existence, and still flourishes. Nor must I fail to acknowledge my indebtedness to Mr. Chas. E. Timms, the indefatigable secretary of the Association of Gramophone and Musical Instrument Manufacturers and Wholesale Dealers, for his admirable account of the foundation, rise and progress of his association ; a most worthy contribution.

OGILVIE MITCHELL.

1 MITRE COURT,
FLEET STREET, E.C.4.

"His Master's Voice"

The best music
recorded by the
greatest Artistes can
only be obtained on

"His Master's Voice"

Gramophone Records

The Gramophone Co., Ltd.
363=367 Oxford Street, London, W.1

CONTENTS

ILLUSTRATIONS

xiii

THE TALKING MACHINE INDUSTRY

CHAPTER I

A HISTORICAL SURVEY

TALKING machine is by no means an ideal name for an invention which is now recognized by the most competent authorities as a true musical instrument. It is, however, the most comprehensive term which has yet been found, for it embraces every type of apparatus that has, up to now, been employed in the reproduction of sound. Talking, indeed, is but a minor function of the mechanism used at present, but it is not at all improbable that the future will witness wider developments in an educational direction which will render this somewhat incongruous name more applicable. In the United States of America the talking machine has been for some years an important factor in the education of the young. There is scarcely a school from Maine to New Orleans or from New York to San Francisco into which the gramophone or phonograph has not been introduced. Later, in its proper place in our handbook, this aspect of the invention will be discussed.

In the earliest ages primitive man was imbued with the notion that inanimate objects could at times give forth vocal utterance, and among remote savage tribes at the present day the belief still holds good. By its means the medicine man and the witch doctor impose upon the less astute members of the community. In like manner the sibyls and soothsayers of antiquity duped the populace. The world-old spurious tales of the voices of the gods, commanding and threatening from rocks, caverns and waterfalls, were foisted upon the believers, and the cunning ones waxed fat and prosperous. The belief in such manifestations was universal, and the truth of them accepted as incontrovertible.

There is no record that the Sphinx ever spoke, but modern excavations in the interior of that strange monument of the past have revealed that, from a chamber in the head, it might have been quite possible for the priests to have answered the questions put by an expectant multitude by means of a megaphone or some such sound amplifying contrivance.

From that mysterious land of Egypt comes the first corroborated account of vocal sound issuing from a thing without life. More than 1,500 years before the beginning of the Christian era there existed an Egyptian monarch named Thothmes III, who had a son Amenophis III, of the XVIIIth Dynasty, who ruled from the Nile to the Euphrates. Besides being a great ruler, Amenophis was a great builder, and founded Luxor, the Egyptian Thebes. He also added largely to Karnak. Possibly he might be identified with the Memnon, Prince of Ethiopia, who went to the aid of the Trojans against the Greeks and was slain by Achilles, but this is mere speculation, and has nothing to do with our survey. At Thebes a mighty temple was erected, with twin colossi at the gates carved out of black basalt. It is certainly strange that in the Greek heroic story Memnon is spoken of as black, and his head after death is said to have prophesied, thus giving ground for the supposition that the Trojan ally and the Egyptian Pharoah were identical ; but again we are straying. One of the colossal statues at Thebes has been from time immemorial denominated Memnon, which would possibly be the Greek form of Amenophis, and from the head of this statue at dawn issued strange sounds. It was not, however, until the Roman occupation of Egypt that we get any distinct description of the character of the noises. Strabo heard them in company with Aelius Gallus and several of his friends, while Pausanias says, one would compare the sound more nearly to the broken chord of a harp or lute. Juvenal and Tacitus also refer to the " vocal Memnon." These are all fairly credible authorities, so that we must not dismiss the ancient story with a sneer. Our own Byron did not, for he sings of " The Ethiop King whose statue turns a harper once a day." From the description by Pausanias we find that the sounds were more musical than articulate. The statue, which was shattered by an earthquake 27 B.C., was restored A.D. 174, but whether the workmen engaged upon the restoration removed the vocal mechanism or destroyed some portion of the head from which the sounds proceeded, will never be known. All that can be said is that, since the latter year, the bust has maintained a discreet silence.

Many theories have been advanced to account for the sonorous property of old Memnon, but all have failed to supply a satisfactory solution. The most probable, in our estimation, would be that the early morning breeze acted upon some hollow in the head and so produced the harp-like twanging which attracted the attention of listeners. In restoring the statue this hollow may have been blocked up.

From Egypt to China is a long step, yet, if we are to trace things in their proper chronological order, it is to the latter country that we must now wing our way. The path may be faint and shadowy, and the light

2—(1466E)

but a weak glimmer, yet we shall follow it as faithfully as we can.

The Chinese seem to have developed a totally independent civilization. Cut off as they were by huge mountain ranges, vast deserts and wide ocean gulfs from the gradually progressive races of Western Asia and the Eastern Mediterranean, they set to work to build up among themselves a system of culture which differed entirely from that of other nations then slowly emerging out of the dark. Their language, their customs, their religion (Ancestor worship is believed to have been the original teaching until Taoism, Confucianism and Buddhism arrived) had no connection whatsoever with Western evolution. They were the same two thousand years ago as they were until Europeans in the middle of the last century pierced the bulwarks the Yellow Man had erected against the rest of the world. Even to the present day the bulk of the population remain adverse to foreign interference. Yet, in arts and several of the sciences, the Chinese were in early days much in advance of the Westerner. They lay claim to having had a knowledge of various inventions and discoveries long before these became the property of other peoples What wonder, then, that the talking machine, when it appeared, was regarded by the Chinaman with his inscrutable smile.

Sir Robert Hart, than whom no Englishman ever understood China with greater comprehension, having spent the best part of his life there in an official capacity, relates the following story. Fifty years before the first talking machine was seen in Pekin, he was one day in conversation with Kwang Tung, the Governor of that city. This Peacock-feather Mandarin was a very learned pundit, well versed in all the lore of his country, and he informed Sir Robert that an ancient book, some two thousand years old, contained the record of a most curious box. At least a thousand years before the book was written a certain Chinese prince was in the habit of communicating with another, who lived in a district far apart. It was necessary that this correspondence should be kept secret, so the prince spoke his messages into a strange box which he sent by a trusty bearer to his distant friend. When this friend opened the box, he could actually hear the voice of the prince speaking the words that had been originally spoken so far away. It must be remembered that the conversation between Kwang Tung and Sir Robert Hart took place before the talking machine, as we know it, was invented. The tale is almost uncanny, but the word of Sir Robert is not to be doubted. Had the Chinese evolved the secret of the talking machine three thousand years before it was dreamt of by Cros or Edison ?

We must now travel long ages through the misty corridors of time before we gain intelligence of any further reproduction of vocal sound. In the thirteenth century lived Roger Bacon, the famous Franciscan monk, He was an Englishman, born in Worcestershire, who studied at Oxford, and there can be little doubt he was a man far in advance of his age. By his strictures on the pretentious ignorance of his fellow monks he incurred the bitter hatred of the Church, and was imprisoned for fourteen years in France. Many important discoveries and inventions are attributed to him, but not all of them on a solid basis of fact. Gunpowder, for instance, was said to have been invented by him, whereas it was known to the Arabs who got it from China, before his day. However, with that we have nothing to do.

Among other mechanical contrivances with which he has been credited was the construction of a talking machine. It was said to have spoken three words and then relapsed into silence, which it could not be induced again to break. In those superstitious days it was no wonder that he was denounced as having been in league with the Evil One, for the devil at that period was given a good deal more than his due. We are afraid, however, that the story is apocryphal, for the *Encyclopaedia Britannica* tells us that careful research has shown that very little in the department of mechanical discovery can with accuracy be ascribed to him. So much, then, for the Roger Bacon tale.

Albertus Magnus, Provincial of the Dominicans at Cologne in the thirteenth century, is also credited with the construction of a brazen head that spoke. It is told that he worked at it for forty years and that then it was smashed to atoms by his more famous pupil, St. Thomas Aquinas, who committed the act in order to show to the world the futility of man's labour, when in one minute he could destroy that which had taken the greater part of a lifetime to build up.

Some three hundred years later one Vaucanson put together a famous duck which attracted extraordinary attention. This curious automaton quacked like the live bird, flapped its wings, gobbled grain and performed various other feats which drew crowds to witness its vagaries. It was, of course, nothing more than a mechanical toy, but four hundred years ago it was a wonder of the world.

This Vaucanson, who was a Parisian of good birth, was a most ingenious fellow, for, besides the duck, he contrived a mechanical flute-player nearly 6 ft. in height. The figure held the instrument to its lips and moved the fingers upon the stops while the flute gave forth familiar airs. We are not informed where the breath came from, but probably it was supplied by some bellows arrangement like that employed by Faber in his speaking automaton of 1860.

Then, in 1632, came a remarkable prototype of the fabulous Baron Munchausen. This was a ship captain, named Vasterlock, who had sailed the southern seas as far as the Straits of Magellan and had a marvellous yarn to tell. He related, with solemn countenance, that the natives of that stormy region grew a wonderful sponge, which, when spoken into, retained in its cells the voice of the speaker. To reproduce the speech one had only to squeeze the sponge and the accents were heard distinctly. Such was the ignorance of the period that many persons actually believed him.

The real Cyrano de Bergerac, who was a living personage, a poet and author of remarkable ability and genius, and not the fictitious hero of a play, as too many who have recently witnessed a very fine performance have been apt to suppose—the real Cyrano, in his book *L' Histoires Comiques des Etats de la Lune*, published in 1654, shadowed forth an instrument which came very close in description to our modern talking machine. Poor de Bergerac was a man of vast imagination, and had he combined it with constructive power, we might have had gramophones two hundred and fifty years ago.

There is a curious story which we read in an American paper not long since, but have been unable to verify. It concerns John Wesley, the eminent founder of the religious sect bearing his name, and, if true, would show that a big stride had been taken in his time towards the production of vocal sounds by mechanical means. Wesley was on one of his long preaching tours, and had crossed to Ireland. In a small town of the West he came upon a poor clock-maker, who showed him an extraordinary timepiece that the man had constructed with his own hands. Instead of striking the hours, it announced them in deep, sonorous tones exactly like the sound of a human voice. The preacher marvelled greatly, and asked the man why he had not exploited his invention. The reply was that poverty prevented him, he had not even the means to purchase the materials to produce another clock on the same lines. Wesley gave him all the money he could spare, which was not much, and rode away. A few years later the great preacher was in Ireland again, and looked up his old friend the clock-maker. Alas ! there was a great change. Sunk into abject misery, his hopes, which had once been high, had given place to despair. The clock was there, but utterly ruined by neglect, and the old man's mind was tottering on the verge of collapse. Sadly Wesley left him, and that is how the story ends. If true, it is only another instance of the futility of genius unassisted by substantial means.

Towards the end of the eighteenth century there appears to have been something very like a craze for the imitation of human speech by mechanical methods. In 1779 an inventor named Kratzenstein produced a machine by which the vowel sounds were automatically pronounced. This was accomplished by forcing air through a reed into different hollows or cavities of varying size   It does not seem, however, to have been a great success.

A more ingenious affair was that of Kempelin, which attracted the attention of Sir David Brewster, who, by the way, was the first man to prophesy that, eventually, a medium for the artificial production of speech would be discovered. Kempelin's invention was more elaborate than that of Kratzenstein. Based very much on the same principle, it was restricted to a single cavity dexterously acted upon by the hand.

Subsequently it was improved until it could be made to pronounce a whole sentence. The words have not been vouchsafed to us, but we suspect they were rather crude in tone and articulation.

The most perfect vocal automaton ever produced was, undoubtedly, that of Faber, who completed it in 1860. This marvellous machine was constructed on anatomical lines analogous to those governing the production of the human voice. The lungs were represented by a keyboard in the trunk, from which air was forced through tubes in the throat to play upon ivory reeds which took the place of the vocal chords. In the larynx a small wheel was inserted to control the roll of the R, and a rubber tongue, with lips of the same material, enunciated the consonants. It was a triumph of mechanical skill, but from what we have read regarding it, the sounds it gave forth were utterly unlike those of anything human.

From all that we can gather this was the last attempt made to imitate the speech of mankind by an artificial device. For several centuries persons had been striving to produce vocal sounds to mimic the voice of nature in man or the lower animals. The idea of reproduction of sound had never occurred to a single soul, though it was strange that the echo, which had fastened upon the minds of the old Greeks, had not taken a grip of later thinkers. In the echo is the actual basis of the talking machine, for it is the sound-wave impinging upon a substance and being thrown back therefrom, while, by the recording process, the wave is seized upon and held for future reproduction.

CHAPTER II

WHAT is sound ? Asked suddenly in a company of ordinary middle-class people we doubt if the question would be immediately answered. The same result would most likely ensue were a similar query propounded in regard to sight, taste or smell, but as sound is the subject on which we are at present engaged we will pursue that alone. The correct answer to the inquiry would be that sound is a sensation produced by the vibratory impact of the air upon the external tympanum, or drum, of the ear, whence it is conveyed by an internal process to the brain. By no possibility could the sound be heard without the air or some less important body acting as a medium. As far back as 1705, Hawksbee made experiments which proved this. In a vacuum the sound of a bell could not be heard. Water is a much better conductor than air, but the atmosphere by which we are constantly surrounded, being the body most easily and most conveniently set in motion, is the unfailing means of exciting that sensation which we call sound. We now perceive that there can be no sound without motion. Take an ordinary glass and strike it with some hard substance so that it gives forth an audible note, then, very gently bring your finger into contact with the rim and you will feel a tremor as long as the sound lasts. If, however, you press your finger upon the edge, so as to stop the vibration, the sound ceases. It is a very simple illustration, but it conveys almost all that need be said on this branch of the subject.

Air is entirely composed of myriads upon myriads

10

of particles, and when these atoms are agitated they jostle each other and, in a greater or less degree, form themselves into wavelets. It is not necessary to bring forward the oft-quoted simile of the stone thrown

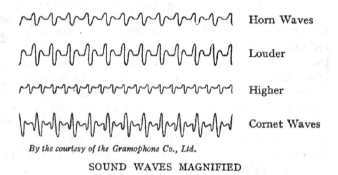

Horn Waves

Louder

Higher

Cornet Waves

By the courtesy of the Gramophone Co., Ltd.

SOUND WAVES MAGNIFIED

into the pond causing ripples to illustrate this simple fact. Chladni, whose *Treatise on Acoustics* was published in Paris in 1809, demonstrated the unerring formation of sound waves by scattering sand on metal

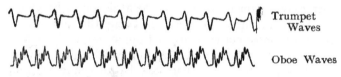

Trumpet Waves

Oboe Waves

By the courtesy of the Gramophone Co., Ltd.

SOUND WAVES MAGNIFIED

plates and subjecting it to the vibrations caused by harmonious notes struck on musical instruments. Tyndall in his Lectures on Sound informs us that a somewhat similar experiment was performed by Lichtenberg before Chladni's time. An electrified powder and resin cakes were used, and the disposition of the powder showed the effect of the electricity upon the surface of the cakes.

About the same date as Chladni, Duhamel was engaged upon experiments which made the nearest approach to the phonograph that had then been discovered. This earnest worker found it practicable to record the sonorous signs by means of a revolving cylinder and papers smeared with lamp-black. A little later the Duc de Leon, in his letters, supported the claim of a German artisan to have successfully reproduced

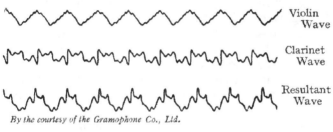

Violin Wave

Clarinet Wave

Resultant Wave

By the courtesy of the Gramophone Co., Ltd.

SOUND WAVES MAGNIFIED

By adding together the violin and clarinet waves we get the resultant wave which the ear receives and analyses

the human voice by mechanical means. That is all we know about it, however, no further reference to the machine having been found. Another step towards reproduction of sound was made by Eisenmanger, of Paris, who, in 1836, secured an English patent for registering pianoforte music by the use of carbonized paper and a depressed stylus.

Inventors were now getting warm, as the children say in their game. The hidden secret of reproduction was being tracked down, but it was still elusive.

Twenty years after Eisenmanger's invention, M. Leon Scott de Martinville came very close to it with his device, " The Phonautograph." Scott was a descendant of one of those intense Jacobites who had followed the unhappy fortunes of King James II, when he fled to France and cast himself on the bounty of the French monarch. Few—some say only one—of those misguided Scotsmen ever returned, and it is certain that Scott's ancestor never did, for the family for generations had been recognized as purely French. Following up Duhamel's discovery of half a century before, this Frenchman with the Caledonian name evolved his "Phonautograph," but being pressed for money, as so many inventors are, he formed a partnership with one Kœnig, who provided the sinews of war.

For a description of Scott's machine we will quote . from our friend Mr. Henry Seymour's valuable work entitled *The Reproduction of Sound*—

"The method employed by Scott was to support a roller, having an extended spindle through its centre and forming its axis, upon two standards or supports, one extension of the spindle being furnished with a thread to engage with a corresponding female thread in one of the standards. A small handle attached to one end of the spindle enabled the drum to be revolved at any desired speed, the traverse movement to provide clearance being, of course, provided by the threaded spindle. The drum was covered with a sheet of paper, the surface of which was prepared with lamp-black ; and at the perimeter of the same was placed a diaphragm of parchment held by a short piece of brass tube, upon one end of which it was stretched in the fashion of a drum-head, the other end of the tube being connected to a focusing chamber or barrel, made from plaster of Paris. Upon the centre of the flexible diaphragm was fixed with sealing wax a stubby hog's bristle ; when the drum was revolved the bristle was in intimate contact with its carbonized surface, and removed the particles of lamp-black with which it came in contact, leaving a distinct marking. It was found when no sound was directed into the barrel or focusing chamber, and the drum was revolved at any speed, only a straight line was marked upon the paper ; but when the drum was revolved at a given speed and sounds of various characters were concentrated in the direction of the flexible diaphragm, the marking or line would assume a wave-like form, and that these peculiar sinuosities varied in size and frequency as the sounds of speech differed in character. In fine, the waves varied with the pitch and intensity of the sound, but were invariably constant for the same sound."

Here, then, was a complete machine for the recording of the human voice, but it lacked the means of reproduction. The voice was there on the paper, but it could not be sent back through the plaster of Paris chamber. You could see the voice but you could not hear it   The *Encyclopaedia Britannica* states that the screw for the traverse movement was the invention of Kœnig, but as Scott and he were jointly engaged upon the work, and Scott had constructed the machine before Kœnig had anything to do with it, we may take it that the credit for the whole should belong to the original inventor.

At a meeting of the British Association in 1859, the Phonautograph was exhibited and attracted a good deal of attention. The Prince Consort was then President of the Association and took a great interest in the machine, demonstrating it to Queen Victoria, who was equally interested.

Although nothing actually useful came from the invention of Scott at the time, it turned the minds of scientists in a new direction, and the vibratory diaphragm was taken up and experimented upon by those with some knowledge of acoustics. Among others was Philip Reiss, of Friedrichsdorf, who proved that the voice could be transmitted from one diaphragm to another by means of an electrified wire conveying a current. This was the first crude telephone. A Scotsman, Alexander Graham Bell, working on the same lines as Reiss, made several wonderful advances, while Gray and others effected some important improvements, until the telephone as we see it to-day came into being. One development followed another, and there can be no question that from the telephone sprang the phonograph.

In regard to the coining of the word " phonograph," we believe the credit is due to a Mr. Fenby, who, in 1863, took out a patent for the electrical recording and reproducing of sound, and registered his instrument by that name. What became of this invention we cannot tell, but most probably it went into that limbo which is specially reserved for the countless products of clever men's brains. Mr. Seymour tells us that it was altogether different in conception and function from the Edison machine.

And now the mention of that magic name leads us on to the great discovery of the secret after which men had been hankering for so many years. There has been considerable dispute in respect to Edison's claim as inventor of the talking machine. Certain it is that, in April, 1877, M. Charles Cros, of Paris, deposited with the French Academy of Sciences the description of a machine almost identical with that in the specification of the patent which was not applied for by Edison till the following year. The question then arises: Was it possible for Edison to have known of the Cros descrip-tion ? We think not, though many have maintained a contrary opinion. It is a moot point which has never been satisfactorily decided, but we are inclined to believe that the balance of the evidence rests in Edison's favour. Was not the appearance of the star Neptune predicted by two astronomers, French and English, for the same hour, and the prediction made simultaneously ? Were not Darwin and Wallace working on the same lines in biology for years and drawing the same conclusions without either of them knowing it ? When such coincidences have been recorded and confirmed, is it incapable of belief that Cros and Edison could have made a simultaneous discovery ?

There are different stories of how the secret of sound reproduction was revealed, but all of them point to an accident. The most popular tale is that supposed to have been told by Mr. Edison himself. " I was singing to the mouthpiece of a telephone," it runs, " when the vibration of the voice sent the fine steel point into my finger. This set me thinking. If I could record the actions of the point over the same surface afterwards I saw no reason why the thing would not talk. I tried the experiment first on a slip of telegraph paper and found that the point made an alphabet. I shouted the words : ' Halloo ! Halloo ! ' into the mouthpiece, ran the paper back over the steel point, and heard a faint ' Halloo ! Halloo ! ' in return. I there and then determined to make a machine which would work accurately. That's the whole story, and this happened in '77."

Mr. Seymour, in his book already referred to, gives a much more scientific version of the discovery, but it is not necessary to trouble the reader with it here, since it is our endeavour to render our little work as free from abstruse technicalities as possible.

Having arrived at the conclusion that the construction of a talking machine came within the bounds of

probability, Edison lost no time in setting to work upon
it. There can be no doubt he knew all about Leon
Scott's invention, for he began where Scott left off. The
roller or drum principle for making the record was
freely adapted from the phonautograph, and the feed
device, said to have been invented by Kœnig on Scott's
machine, was also used. There, however, to a great
extent, the similarity ended. The means employed to
obtain the record were different. Edison's roller was
spirally grooved, and instead of the paper and lamp-
black previously used, tinfoil was substituted as a
covering for the drum. The hog's bristle on the diaphragm gave place to a steel point which made indentations on the tinfoil when the drum was revolved and
the diaphragm was caused to vibrate by sound. These
indentations were, of course, very minute and followed
the grooves on the roller in irregular fashion, some
deeper than others, with varying distances between,
corresponding with the strength and frequency of the
sounds uttered into the focusing-chamber. When the
needle was again made to traverse the indented path,
reconveying the vibrations to the diaphragm, the
original sounds were reproduced. The great secret was
a secret no longer. The reproduction of the human
voice had been achieved.

At first the sounds were faint and unnatural, but the
enlargement of the focusing-chamber into an amplifying
horn bore its fruit in increased distinctness, nevertheless
the whole comtraption was exceedingly crude. A
detailed description, giving dimensions, runs as follows :
The machine consisted of a brass drum, 4 ins. in length
and 3·4 ins. in diameter, carried on a screw shaft which
advanced ·1 for each revolution. The surface of the
drum was traversed by a narrow groove of ·1 in., and was
covered with tinfoil. At right angles to the axis was

fixed a tube closed at the end nearest the drum by a thin ferrotype plate, which had at its centre a projecting stylus. The vibrations of the plate caused the stylus to indent the unsupported tinfoil as the cylinder revolved. On the opposite side of the drum was another tube, closed at its outer end by a paper diaphragm from the centre of which a light rod passed to a rounded pin, which a spring carried close to the tinfoil surface. On the drum being rotated and the pin brought into contact with the indented foil, the sounds which had caused the vibration of the ferrotype plate were reproduced.

Very soon it was found that the hand-crank gave an irregular motion to the mandril, and Edison cast about for some mechanism which would overcome this. Water and electricity were both tried, the latter being definitely adopted and holding the sway until 1894, when Mr. T. H. Macdonald, the factory manager of the American Graphophone Company, succeeded in producing a clock-work motor   This met with general approval, but was surpassed by a motor previously made in England by the late Mr. Fitch, of Goswell Road, London, a most ingenious invention, with a delicate governing apparatus. It is the model which forms the basis for all the more modern motors used as the driving force for every kind of cylinder machine.

As a man of action Edison hastened to apply for a patent. His claims for the potentialities of his invention are worthy of note : (1) Letter writing and all kinds of dictation without the aid of a stenographer ; (2) Phonographic books, which will speak to blind people without effort on their part ; (3) The teaching of Elocution ; (4) Reproduction of Music , (5) The " Family Record "—a registry of sayings, reminiscences. etc., by members of a family in their own voices, and of

the last words of dying persons ; (6) Music boxes and
toys ; (7) Clocks that should announce in articulate
speech the time for going home, going to meals, etc. ;
(8) The preservation of languages by the exact reproduction of the manner of pronouncing ; (9) Educational
purposes, such as preserving the explanation made by
a teacher, so that the pupil can refer to them at any
moment, and spelling and other lessons placed upon
the machine for convenience in committing to
memory ; and (10) Connection with the telephone so
as to make the invention an auxiliary in the transmission
of permanent and invaluable records, instead of being
the recipient of momentary and fleeting communications.

It is a great list, but application No. 4 seems to be
the only one that so far has been completely carried out.
A curious fact, too, is that he should claim for the teaching of elocution and not for the teaching of music,
whereas to-day there is scarcely a school in America in
which the talking machine is not used for the latter
purpose. In this connection also 'there is a noteworthy
instance of the value of the machine as a teacher.
Madame Galli-Curci, the famous operatic *prima donna*
was refused an engagement by every impresario of
distinction in the States. Her voice was not considered
good enough. Nothing daunted, she went away and
secluded herself with a gramophone and a big parcel
of records made from the voices of the leading *soprani*
of the day. In the peace and quietness of her home
she practised assiduously, testing her voice against
those on the records. Gradually her vocal organ
improved. It had been there all along, but her training
had been insufficient. At last, when she imagined
she was qualified, she presented herself to a manager
asking for an audition. He remembered her and
declined to listen. It was the same with others. They

3—(1466E)

had heard her once and refused to give her another
chance. Almost despairing, she made her way to
Chicago, where, by good fortune, she found a gentleman
who acceded to her request. He listened and was

By the courtesy of the Gramophone Co., Ltd.

MADAME GALLI-CURCI

amazed. She got her engagement at once, and now she
is the idol of America. A talking machine had wrought
a seeming miracle.

In claim No. 8 Edison speaks of the " preservation "
of languages   He may have been thinking of the dying
tongues of the fast disappearing Red Race of his native
country   Certainly the instrument would be of use in
preserving for the knowledge of the curious some
specimens of the speech of those Indians, but we cannot
conceive what benefit that would be to humanity.

America has done her best to destroy the Red Man, why should she wish to preserve his language ? However, in teaching living languages the talking machine has been making great progress of late, and there is a tremendous future before it in this direction. There are other branches of education, too, in which it will presently be found extremely useful, not forgetting our friend the dancing-master, who is installing machines all over the country to provide the necessary music.

The first machine constructed by Edison, a model of which, presented by himself, may be seen in South Kensington Museum (there is a photograph of it hanging before our eyes at the present moment), was a very clumsy affair with a handle for rotating the cylinder and the results were far from satisfactory. Nevertheless, they were a reproduction and gave a basis for further experiment. The tinfoil was not well suited to receive the extremely delicate indentations of the recording needle. It offered too great a resistance, and the consequence was that the sounds were feeble and indistinct even after the enlargement of the focusing-chamber, so rubber tubes had to be used to convey the sounds from the diaphragm to the ear. The public, after the first burst of wonderment at the novelty, did not regard it with much favour. In the eyes of the average man it was nothing more than a scientific toy.

CHAPTER III

IT had taken just upon seventy years, from the time of Duhamel's Vibrograph to the imperfect phonograph of Edison, for the reproduction of sound to be achieved. In the meantime both the telegraph and the telephone had been launched upon the world, but these were of an electric nature, whereas the talking machine had nothing whatsoever to do with electricity. It was an exceedingly simple contrivance based upon the storage and release of sound by means of vibrations, and its utility in the beginning was doubtful.

In the same year that Edison filed his application in the United States, 1878, he took out an English patent, No. 1644. By this it may be seen to the present day that he did not pin his faith solely to tinfoil as a recording medium. He mentions also waxes, gums or lacs, but at that time he undoubtedly believed in what is commonly known as " silver paper."

Whether Edison was disheartened by the comparative failure of his invention or was too busily engaged with other novelties which promised to be more remunerative we have no knowledge, but it is an undisputed fact that for about ten years he allowed his work upon the instrument to fall into abeyance. There were others, however, almost as keen-witted as himself, who were striving eagerly to produce a device which would not infringe the Edison American patent. These men were that indefatigable Scotsman, Alexander Graham Bell, whose name has already been mentioned in connection with the telephone, his brother, Chichester Bell, and a clever American scientist, Charles Sumner Tainter. While Edison was dreaming or toiling in other directions, these three were ferreting out fresh secrets in regard to the phonograph. Unaware of the original inventor's English patent, which mentioned wax as a recording medium, they discovered that by the employment of a composition which had wax as its principal ingredient they had a workable substance. They discarded the steel point used by Edison and substituted a sapphire stylus shaped like a gouge. This latter dug into the wax " blank," as the mandril coating was called (a term now used for all kinds of surfaces upon which sounds are recorded in the first instance), instead of merely indenting as the needle had done upon the tinfoil. To the instrument constructed by the trio they gave the name of "Graphophone," a name still used by the highly successful Columbia Company for their machines. The results obtained by the Bell and Tainter method of recording were greatly in advance of those secured by the Edison, and an interest in the talking machine was at once re-awakened. In one respect the new invention remained the same as the original. The track made by the stylus on the wax, like that made by the pin-head on the tinfoil, was of the " hill-and-dale " or undulating variety. The sinuous or zigzag track was still in the air, so to speak.

The success of the Graphophone in the reproduction of sound led capitalists to look upon it in the light of a commercial proposition. Companies were formed to manufacture machines and records, and to exploit them to the world. In fact, there arose a boom in the invention which that of Edison had never known, and records of the voices of popular American vocalists sold throughout the States as rapidly as they could be turned out.

In the beginning every one of these records was a " master," that is to say, it was the original as it was slipped off the cylinder, but soon a duplicating machine was manufactured by which copies could be taken without injury to the master. This machine has now almost fallen into desuetude, and the cylinder record is fast following it into the region of forgotten things. At that time, however, it was in full swing, and the copies made by it had the inevitable effect of cheapening the market.

The vogue of the Graphophone aroused Edison and caused him once more to turn his mind to the talking machine. Immediately the fat was in the fire. As Tainter and Bell had adopted Edison's mandril and cylinder without saying by your leave, so Edison fastened upon their cutting apparatus Both parties appealed to the law and fought their hardest. Edison maintained that indenting was equivalent to cutting, Tainter and Bell asserted that it was a different process altogether. The suit dragged on interminably, and the costs mounted higher and higher, and all the time it was giving the talking machine bold advertisement. The law's delay is quite as notorious in America as it is here, if not more so, and people began to whisper that the continued prolongation of the actions was caused by the desire of the litigants to deter other inventors from entering into a field fraught with so many terrors. The end of it all was—a dollar ! Each paid the other this magnificent sum for infringement of patent and peace was proclaimed. What the costs amounted to nobody but those concerned in the case ever knew.

The immediate effect of the drawn battle was the formation of a company called the Edison United, which bought the patents that had been the *casus belli*, and fondly imagined they had got hold of everything and there would be no more litigation. However, no sooner had this new concern found its feet and was doing great business than the former foes came together and promoted the Edison-Bell Company, a name still perpetuated by J. E. Hough, Ltd., of Glengall Road, Peckham, London. How this firm became entitled to the use of the famous name is too long a story to be related here, but it was acquired by perfectly legitimate means. As it was, after a time Edison became dissatisfied with the way the company was carrying on business, though his name still appeared in conjunction with that of Bell in the title of the company, as it does to this day.

Before the first talking machine war had ignominiously fizzled out, however, a new method of obtaining records from the " master " had been discovered which revolutionized the whole business. The old duplicating process was superseded by electrotyping. By this means the master was covered with a coating of copper and any number of moulded copies could be taken from it without difficulty. Though Edison was not the inventor of this system he vastly improved upon it, and the records, by reason of the use of harder wax, and consequently the more exact reproduction of the voice, became much more marketable. Later on other metals than copper were employed, and under the vacuum deposit process, which reduces metals to a vapour by high tension electric currents, gold moulded cylinder records made their appearance. The enormous quantities which were produced again brought down the price and the public demand increased.

Hitherto, it will be observed, that we have spoken solely and entirely of America from the time that

Edison took out his first patent. The reason for this is not difficult to trace. There were no talking machines anywhere else. The patent holders had a monopoly of them, they were not permitted to be exported except under licence, and this licence was granted to nobody unless contracts were signed of the most one-sided character. The story of how the first phonograph was smuggled across the Atlantic to Ireland is most interesting and amusing, and we give it straight from the mouth of the gentleman who perpetrated the deed. He is alive and flourishing to-day, and is still connected with the talking machine trade. His name is Mr. Percy Willis, and he is sales manager to the firm of J. E. Hough, Ltd , already mentioned, whose Winner records are known all over the world.

" Well, I won't say that ours was absolutely the first machine on this side," said Mr. Willis when we saw him at the Edison Bell Works in Peckham, " but I'll swear it was the first to be smuggled, and they were smuggled in their thousands afterwards. We had been doing rotten business in Canada, my partner and I, and cash was running short. When one feels the lining of his wallet wearing thin it sharpens his wits and brightens up his intellect. Anyhow, I've always found it so, and I've had a pretty wide experience. We were in Montreal, and one evening as we passed down the street we came upon a sort of booth or curtained store where a great crowd of people were hovering around. Outside there was a big bill posted up announcing that a phonograph might be heard within at so many cents a head. ' Gee,' ! I exclaimed. ' If we could only get one of these machines and a few dozen records across to England our fortunes would be made.' I may tell you, at that time the Edison United was controlling the earth in the talking machine line. They had little or no opposition, for Berliner had not then taken out his patents, and this company was running the Edison and the Tainter and Bell inventions combined in one.   They were the lords of creation in the new business, and they carried things with a mighty high hand.   My partner agreed with me that there was money in the notion, and we made up our minds to go ahead without delay.

"Next day we took train for Boston, and there we bought the machine and three dozen cylinder records.   For these we had to put our names to several portentous looking documents, binding us down to all kinds of restrictions, the most important of which, to us, was that neither the machine nor the records were to be taken out of the United States under a penalty of something approaching to electro- cution.   But what did we care ?   We had determined upon the adventure and we would take all risks.   By the time we had paid for our passages from Boston to Queenstown we were just about the end of our tether so far as cash went, but we were buoyed up with plenty of hope for the future.   We were precious careful of our baggage, I can assure you, for on that depended the whole of our expectations.   However, we got through to Queenstown all right and then—I'll never forget it ! We were going ashore when the strap supporting the parcel of records broke and there was a crash.   My heart was in my mouth, but when we came to examine we found that only twelve of them had gone, we had still a couple of dozen to carry on with.

"Of course, it was necessary for us to see about business at once.   We could not afford to rest on our oars for a single moment, so we made our start there and then in Queenstown, and a splendid start it was.   The people came rolling in by dozens and scores.   In those days, you know, to hear the record you had to listen with tubes in your ears, and there was no spring motor to drive the machine. The mandril was rotated by electricity which necessitated lugging a battery about with you. These were drawbacks which have all been overcome long since, but the thing was then in its swaddling clothes and hadn't even begun to crawl. The worst of it was that only one person could listen at a time and, especially with children, there was a good deal of difficulty in subduing the impatience of the waiting crowd.

" From the very first day of our opening I saw that most of our anticipations were to be fulfilled. Everybody was full of the wonderful talking machine and our fame preceded us to Cork which was our next town. There they flocked to us in shoals, and I recollect one old woman standing with a market basket on her arm while I expatiated on the wonders of the invention. She regarded me with a wistful eye for a long time, and then in an audible whisper she asked a neighbour, ' What's ailin' him ? '

" Waterford and Limerick were little gold mines to us, and then we opened at the Central Hall in Dublin. In the first five days we took £200. Our dreams were being realized, and there were not two happier fellows in the whole of Ireland.

" While in Dublin we had a private visit from the Lord Mayor of the city, who brought three members of Parliament with him. They had come especially to hear the voice of Gladstone, who was then in extraordinary favour with the Irish because of his Home Rule Bill. Now, I was just a little perturbed about this. We had a record of the words of Gladstone giving his famous message to Edison on the marvel of the talking machine, but the voice—well, it was not the actual voice of the great statesman, it was that of somebody else. In fear and trembling I put it on. Each of the visitors heard it in turn with reverential awe. Then, judge of my surprise when one of them grasped me by the hand.   ' Thank you, sir,' he remarked, ' I have sat behind the old man for nearly fifty years and recognize every tone of the voice.'   I guess the man who made that record must have been a great mimic.

" We did so well in Dublin that I thought I would chance another smuggling expedition to the States for more records and a few machines, for we had had many inquiries concerning the price of them and how they could be obtained. I went and was entirely successful, bringing the goods over in apple barrels packed as fruit. We were now in full swing. The machines sold for high prices to persons who wished to enter into the same line as ourselves and the entertainment business flourished exceedingly. I remember a very amusing incident, though it was rather serious at the moment. We were going from Ireland to the Isle of Man, for the season in Douglas   As I have already told you, we had to carry an electric battery with us for the motor power to turn the cylinder. While waiting for the boat in Liverpool I had the battery fully charged ready to start as soon as we reached the island. The terminals were on top. and I set the thing down and walked away for a minute or two. In my absence a woman came along with a tin box and flopped it atop of my apparatus. The box being of metal completed the circuit, and by the time I returned the bottom of that box had gone and the lady thought she had struck an infernal machine. I had to recompense her, of course, which, I suppose, served me right for my carelessness.

" At that time Charles Coborn was at his zenith with ' The Man Who Broke the Bank at Monte Carlo.'   We contrived to get a record of the song, and it was one of the greatest hits we ever made.   People used to come again and again to listen to it, and then they would bring their friends.   Everybody wanted to hear that song, till at last the cylinder got clean worn out, for in those days the wax that they were made of was rather soft stuff and wouldn't last as the later cylinders did.

" It was a glorious life and I enjoyed myself amazingly. There were other trips to America, each one more profitable than the last, and I was never caught; though once one of the Edison United men came after me on this side and wanted to know the names of the parties who had machines from me.   I refused to give him any information and defied him.   He had no proofs against me, in spite of the fact being known that I was engaged in that sort of contraband ; but there were certain prosecutions of other persons, and one of the best known men in the trade since then was obliged to take refuge in Holland for a time.

" Those days are long past now.   The high-handed methods of the Edison United have departed from these shores, and the gramophone has almost entirely taken the place of the phonograph.   When my partner— alas ! he is dead now, poor fellow—and I severed our connection he got the highest price ever paid for a talking machine up till that time.   It was the good old instrument that had lasted us all through, and he sold it for £200 !   Our records, too, fetched a pound a piece."

CHAPTER IV

THE DISC MACHINE

IT has been previously stated that the gramophone, or disc machine, has, in this country at least, practically ousted the older invention from the English market. Up to the outbreak of the war with Germany, Edison had a big factory at Willesden, on the northern outskirts of London, and did a fairly good, though declining, trade. At one time, of course, he had had almost a monopoly of the industry in England, and the Edison machine was the popular instrument. There are still a certain number of enthusiasts clinging to it scattered throughout the country, who have formed societies of their own and endeavour to revive the dying cult, but we fear that their success is limited. Some of the trade factors, that is to say, the wholesalers, have accused the Edison Company in Britain of sharp practice. The American methods of business did not suit the slower-moving traders of this country and there were latterly some actions at law. The Edison factory closed down and there were no more cylinders or machines on sale from that quarter. It is not improbable that the managers of the British branch of the business formed a wrong estimate of the effect the war would have upon the trade and scuttled off to avoid a slump. If that should have been the case, they made the biggest mistake of their lives, for the war proved to be of the greatest benefit to the trade generally, from the manufacturer down to the humblest dealer, although it was almost entirely in favour of the disc machine. Nevertheless, had the

31

Edison people stuck to their guns they would, in all likelihood, have had a share in the prosperity. In the whole of the three kingdoms there is now but one small factory turning out cylinders, that of the Clarion Company, at Wandsworth.

The inventor of the disc system was Emil Berliner It will be remembered that both the Edison and the Tainter-Bell processes were those of the hill and dale track, Berliner reverted to the old method of Leon Scott with his phonautograph, and produced a sinuous or zigzag pathway. This is known to experts as the needle-cut record, while the original is the phono-cut. Berliner's first essay in disc reproduction was to coat a flat zinc plate with a viscous film, as is done in zincography, and then to engrave thereon by means of a needle attached to a diaphragm the sinuosities resulting from the sound-imparted vibrations of the diaphragm. These appeared as tiny microscopical wriggles running in a spiral track on the face of the prepared disc, which were afterwards bitten into the zinc by acid. To obtain a reproduction a vertical diaphragm was used which had a stylus supported by a lever and acted upon by a point which ran in the concentric grooves. After being engraved the zinc disc was employed for the purpose of procuring a metallic negative from which countless records could be pressed in a composition consisting mainly of shellac, which hardens when cold. The reproductions thus obtained were, however, rough and crude, and recourse was afterwards had to the wax blank and the sapphire stylus. For the record made in this latter way a treatment of very fine graphite was applied which metallized it, and the electrotyping went on in the ordinary manner, with a solution of sulphate of copper bath, and the application of a high tension current. Great care had to be exercised in this

By the courtesy of Messrs. Alfred Graham & Co.,
St. Andrew's Works, Crofton Park, London, S.E.

AN ALGRAPHONE

The most elaborately ornate gramophone exhibited at the
British Trade Industries' Fair, 1922

process, and special appliances had to be introduced for the purpose of procuring a good and service-able master from which the working matrices were obtained.

There can be no doubt that the Berliner disc is the favourite upon the market, but there are phono-cut discs as well, which have a considerable following

By the courtesy of the Gramophone Co., Ltd.

HIS MASTER'S VOICE PORTABLE GRAMOPHONE

among gramophone users. Our friend, Mr. Seymour, filed two specifications in reference to the recording and reproduction of this type of disc as far back as 1903, and one Dr. Michaelis, a German, took out a patent in this country a few months later for a somewhat similar invention. The doctor's was a rather curious production in stout strawboard coated with enamel, and faced with celluloid on which the record had been impressed.

He called it the " Neophone," and we saw one of them
not long since in the possession of a collector, who
preserved it as a curio. Some of these discs were huge
affairs, 20 ins. across. As a matter of fact, they were
ultimately a failure. The strawboard warped and the
records became useless.

Undoubtedly the most successful firm in the exploitation of this system are Messrs. Pathé Frères, of Paris,
London and New York, who years ago adopted the
undulating method as applied to discs. Their records
are pressed in the shellac composition like all others of
this form, but have greater durability in consequence
of being played with a ball pointed sapphire which does
not give so much wear and tear as the sharp steel needle.
For the same reason there is not quite so much surface
sound.

Edison himself has now brought out a disc of this
design, but it has not reached England yet. It may,
nevertheless, be expected at any moment, and will
probably be on sale before our little work is in print.
It is played, we are told, by a diamond, but this is
nothing new, Pathé Frères had a diamond reproducer
at the same time as their sapphire, but have now abandoned it in favour of the latter. High encomiums have
been passed on the Edison disc by the inventor's own
countrymen, who praise it for its lack of that besetting
sin of the gramophone, the surface scratch. By the way,
the term " gramophone " was given by Berliner to his
instrument in the same fashion as Edison called his
machine a phonograph and Tainter and Bell named
theirs a graphophone. But more of this hereafter. If
the Edison disc should fulfil all the claims that are made
for it the friends of the talking mahcine will welcome
it with open arms, for even the most ardent admirers
of the instrument cannot disguise from themselves

the fact that in several respects there is room for improvement.[1]

It will no doubt be news to certain of our readers that sound has been photographed, yet a patent for sound photography was granted to Morgan-Brown so far back as 1880. Since then at least half a dozen have followed, including one to the irrepressible Graham Bell, in 1886.

"The principle involved in most of these methods," says Seymour, "is to vary an otherwise constant beam of light passed through a condenser and reflecting upon a small mirror attached to a vibrating diaphragm, the reflected beam or 'light pencil' being directed to impinge upon a blank with a sensitized surface. The recording machine is constructed much upon the same lines as those of the ordinary disc recording machine, with the addition, of course, that it is also a modified camera."

Another plan for obtaining a record is by a somewhat intricate process of passing the record between a concentrated beam of light falling on a selenium cell in circuit with a microphone by which the light waves are converted into sound waves. The system, however, has not yet been perfected. Theoretically the photophone may be all right, but we have not had the pleasure of listening to any of the records so reproduced, and until we do, we are rather inclined to be a little sceptical. That sound has been photographed we

[1] Since writing the above we have had an opportunity of listening to the much-vaunted Edison records on an Edison specially constructed machine, and have been most grievously disappointed. They are formidable looking discs of about a quarter of an inch in thickness, though very light considering, but, instead of diminishing the surface sound, the disagreeable scratch is much more manifest than ever, and in other respects the records show no advantage whatsoever over those at present issued by the best manufacturers The artists, too, both vocal and instrumental, are a poor lot compared with those who are exclusively engaged by some of the other manufacturers.

readily admit, it is the reproduction that we are doubtful about. Were the conjunction of light' and sound brought into complete harmony the synchronization of the kinematograph with the gramophone would not be far distant. And that opens up an entirely new vista which we must not yet dwell upon because we are not gifted with the power of prophecy ; nevertheless, it is our opinion that before long the camera and the talking machine will come into consonance, so that we shall hear the voices of the players on the screen as well as witness their actions.

We remember an attempt was made by Edison some years ago to synchronize the bioscope with the phonograph, and a private show was given at the Company's premises in Clerkenwell Road, London. It was a ghastly failure. The mouths of the characters opened, but no words came, and, *vice versa*, when the lips were closed the machine persisted in talking. It was simply ludicrous. Since then, we understand, Edison has still been working on the idea but has not arrived at a satisfactory result. However, other inventors are pegging away at it, and quite recently we heard that Sir Harry Lauder has secured something wonderful in this line which he is keeping up his sleeve.[1]

[1] The latest news from America assures us that the synchronization of the talking machine and the film has been achieved by means of the endless band. The method of producing a record upon a celluloid tape is not new. It was suggested several years ago though never actually carried out. Celluloid as a record substance goes back for a long time. As we have already noted Dr. Michaelis used it for his Neophone, and Edison's " Blue Amberols," the best cylinder records ever manufactured, were of this material. Celluloid or cellulose may be fashioned in flexible form and the record impressed upon it. A long ribbon of this could easily embody a whole opera, the reproduction being effected by passing the band over a couple of mandrils. In the timing of it with the film the record and the picture are reeled off together, so that the action and the voice correspond exactly. It is an ingenious notion, and we trust it may fructify.

To revert to the Berliner disc machine or gramophone. It was patented in the year 1887, but not for another decade was it freely sold in Great Britain, though a few had made their appearance from America. Up till then the only machine known in this country was the cylinder. About 1897, Berliner sold his English patent rights to a private concern which called itself after the name of the instrument, The Gramophone Company. This firm dealt in talking machines made under the patent which they had purchased from the inventor ; but in 1899 it transferred the business to a company incorporated under the style of The Gramophone Company, Limited. A year later this company, in its turn, transferred the concern to a company with a much larger capital, which had at the same time acquired a business in typewriters, and was known as The Gramophone and Typewriter, Limited. Shortly afterwards it dropped its typewriter interest and became again The Gramophone Company, Limited, a title which it still retains.

In 1900 the Tainter-Bell patent expired, and this was followed some time later by the expiration of the Berliner 1887 patent. In less than no time 'phones of all kinds were being rushed upon the public. Many of these were given fancy names, such as " Dulcephone," " Coronophone," and the like, but not one of them was known as a " Gramophone." That name was believed to be sacred to The Gramophone Company alone, and the mushroom manufacturers—many of them, in fact, most of them, Germans—had a wholesome dread of treading upon the corns of a corporation which was rapidly making its presence felt.

The first double-sided disc was introduced to this country from Germany in 1904, and was a very good record indeed, which cannot be said of all its congeners.

It belonged to the firm of C. and J. Ullmann and was named the Odeon Duplex. Odeon records were much sought after, and even now, with all the outcry against the admission of German goods, there are occasional inquiries for them. They were in two sizes, $7\frac{1}{2}$ ins. and $10\frac{3}{4}$ ins. in diameter.

In the same year also appeared the National Phonograph Company, which was the Edison Company already referred to, with its European headquarters in Holland. The firm opened business in Gray's Inn Road and prospered so well that in a few months it took additional premises at 25 Clerkenwell Road. It then established a big factory at Willesden, London, N.W., and for some years did a flourishing trade. In the end, however, as we have previously stated, it went down, like a good many others, and England knew it no more. This practically severed the last British link with Edison and his phonograph.

It was a year of great events in the Talking Machine Industry that 1904, for it likewise saw the arrival in this country of one of the most successful disc ventures that are known here at the present time. The British Zonophone Company came to London, bringing with it, as manager, a gentleman who is now deservedly regarded as one of the leading lights of the trade. We refer to Mr. Louis Sterling, who has been for several years the Managing Director of the British house of the world famous Columbia Graphophone Company. There is not a scheme for the welfare of the industry and the betterment of its prospects in which Mr. Sterling is not one of the moving spirits, and withal he is so unassuming, so genial, that he has endeared himself to everyone with whom he comes in contact. Still, like most men who have risen from small beginnings, and Mr. Sterling would not be ashamed to tell you himself that his beginnings were very small, he has had his struggles. Resigning his position with the Zonophone Company within a short period, he launched The Sterling Record Company, with a play upon his own name, and was shortly afterwards joined by Mr. Russell Hunting, an adventurous spirit, well known in the gramophone trade throughout the world. Hunting had previously been with the Edison-Bell Consolidated Company, from which he had seceded with a few others, and after joining Mr. Sterling, the name of the latter's concern was changed to the Russell Hunting Co. They occupied the old Zonophone premises at 81 City Road, while the Zono people moved to 23.

The increasing popularity of the disc record was already beginning to affect the cylinder trade, and in 1905 war arose between the Edison-Bell Consolidated Phonograph Company and the National Phonograph Company. We are not quite clear on the merits of the case, but, it seems that the National Company in a trade circular laid claim to the name of Edison as their own exclusive property. They doubtless had some grounds for this as they were working Edison patents, but so were their opponents at the same time. The Edison-Bell at once countered with a heavy stroke. They announced in the clearest terms that " all Edison patents, together with others of importance within the United Kingdom, relating to the modern Phonograph were purchased by the Edison Corporation, Ltd , for the sum of £40,000, and that in the purchase deeds of this transaction it was agreed that the first word of its trading name should be EDISON." The challenge having been thrown down long litigation followed, which did not tend to the enhancement of prosperity in the cylinder trade. In the midst of the turmoil caused by the opposing companies the disc people were strengthening their hands. Factors and dealers were looking this way and that in a state of bewilderment, and presently conceived that their surest hope of salvation lay in the support of the non-combatant. So the disc scored while the Kilkenny cats of the cylinder were tearing each other to death.

It is interesting to observe that about this time there were efforts made to establish a trade in the commercial phonograph. The Edison-Bell Company had already been endeavouring to force the market with their Dictaphone. Then there was registered the Shorthand Record Company, an enterprise which brought out a series of records for dictation purposes in conjunction with the teaching of stenography. The Linguaphone, too, was an instrument designed for the teaching of languages, but the public was not ready for it, and neither of these projects had a very long life. Nowadays, when the desire for the acquirement of foreign tongues has been greatly stimulated by the war, there are being issued quantities of educational discs, and the matter is being taken up in earnest.

The Columbia Company was now forging ahead with fine determination. They had achieved a record of the voice of Pope Leo XIII which was in itself a masterpiece of enterprise, as it ensured the patronage and favour of all good Catholics. That was followed by some remarkable cylinders of the favourite operatic singers of the day, Edouard de Reszke, Scotti, and Campanani, with Mesdames Sembrich and Schumann-Heinck. Not to be outdone, the Gramophone Company, by this time an exceedingly prosperous concern, came out with discs of Caruso, Plançon, Scotti, Madame Calvé, and many others.

During this period more German records were being introduced to the English market in the form of the

Beka, the Dacapo and the Favourite.   The Fonotipia, also came over from Italy, with Messrs C. and J. Ullmann, of the Odeon, as agents.   The records of these companies were all discs and added heavily to the preponderance of the balance in favour of that type.   The records were mostly made here, but the machines marketed by these concerns were all Teutonic, stock, lock and barrel. Indeed, up till that time there were few talking machines of actual British build.

By far the best season that had then been known in the trade since the instrument was brought across the Atlantic was the winter of 1906-7.   Machines and records were plentiful and buyers were many ; but the following two years showed a disastrous reverse.   The reason for this might be found in the unsettled nature of the business owing to the competition between the cylinder and the disc.   The mind of the public was distracted between the types and so they bought neither.   In the general slump the Russell Hunting Company, with its cylinder record, was wound up.   It was perhaps not a bad thing for Mr. Sterling after all, for a little later he introduced a disc record under the name Rena, which was subsequently absorbed by the Columbia, and Louis Sterling found himself at the head of affairs in the whole concern.

CHAPTER V

FROM what has previously been said, it will be understood that the talking machine, so far as it has yet been evolved, requires various appliances and accessories to act in conjunction with it before we can get a perfect reproduction of the recorded sound. In disc machines there must, first of all, be the motor to rotate the record, then the turntable on which the record is placed, after that the point to follow the grooves and transmit the vibrations to the reproducer or sound box, which receives the vibrations from the point and passes them on, as re-embodied sound, to the amplifier to be strengthened in volume and spread abroad. In connection with the horn there is also the tone arm which carries the sound from the reproducer to the amplifying horn, and is a comparatively recent introduction. If we look closely into the trade-mark of the Gramophone Company, the well-known "His Master's Voice" picture, we will see that the sound box is attached to the lower portion of the horn without the intervention of any tubular apparatus. That was the Berliner system when first brought out. There is also in certain gramophones another attachment, known as the gooseneck, which is interposed between the tone arm and the reproducer, but it is of no value beyond that of convenience in placing the needle in its holder and the proper adjustment of the sound box.

Speaking of the motor, we have already stated that the first phonographs were hand-driven, then came electric power, and after that the smoothly running clockwork contrivance. In both types of machine in use at present the actuating power is the steel spring,

and the object to be attained is the noiseless and perfectly steady movement of the delicate machinery.   To
enter into all the minutiae of the apparatus would
necessitate a long and technical dissertation upon the
mechanism which would assuredly prove tedious to the
majority of our readers.   When a man buys a watch
he does not want to learn the whole process of its
manufacture.   All that he wishes to know is whether
it will keep correct time, and so it is with the motor of
a talking machine.   The purchaser only desires to be
assured that it will drive the turntable, or the mandril,
smoothly, steadily, and without noise.   Now, here
comes an extraordinarily characteristic feature of our
English idiosyncrasies.   Having developed the most
perfect device for the driving of the phonograph, in the
shape of the Greenhill motor made by Fitch, we straight-
way allowed it to slip through our fingers into the hands
of somebody else.   It must be premised that the principle of the motor for both the phonograph and the
gramophone is the same, the difference being merely a
matter of design.   When the Tainter-Bell and Berliner
patents expired, and it was seen that the disc was to be
the machine of the future, the Germans set to work upon
it with the concentrated vigour which belongs to them.
It is one of the distinguishing presentments of the
Teutonic brain that it does not originate, but given the
groundwork upon which to labour it will forthwith
produce much fruit of a serviceable nature if not
of a high quality.   The Germans speedily turned out
cheap motors by the thousand, but presently they were
beaten by the Swiss, who, after long generations of
experience in clock and watch making, found the gramophone requirement a comparatively easy proposition.
While these foreigners were busy flooding the
British markets with these products of cheap labour

not a single motor was manufactured in England. Every machine that was built in this country had a foreign motor inside it. This went on until the war put a stop to the influx of German goods and restrictions were placed upon the importation of Swiss wares. It was then that our own manufacturers began to take thought. British handicraft had always been the best in the world. Why had we permitted Germany and

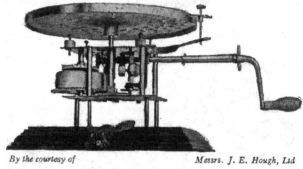

By the courtesy of   *Messrs. J. E. Hough, Ltd*

SINGLE SPRING MOTOR WITH TURNTABLE

Switzerland to supplant us in the matter of talking machine motors? At that time, however, firms that would have started without delay were handicapped for the lack of men. Engineers and artificers were at the front or engaged upon munitions. There was not a craftsman to be had. Nevertheless, several companies were formed by men of foresight, and since demobilization began some of the companies have got to work and are turning out goods that the Germans or Swiss could never compete with. Certain of the bigger machine manufacturers, too, are now constructing their own motors, instead of importing foreign makes, and we hope before long to see every gramophone bearing an English name British made in all its parts.

A visit to one of the new factories is a most interesting experience. It was our privilege not long since to be shown over one of the largest of them, where nothing but gramophone motors are made on the exact principle of mass production—a notable post-war enterprise.

The buildings covered a large area and every department was in full working order. From the store

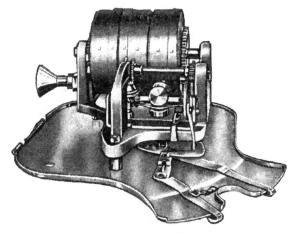

THE TRIPLE-SPRING MOTOR UNIT OF A
COLUMBIA INSTRUMENT

(Shown inverted to display mechanical parts)

at one end bars and sheets of the finest steels were issued into the main factory where a succession of whirring machines absorbed them. Every one of these was attended by highly skilled artificers, and as the metal was passed along it was shaped and cut into all the component parts, spindles, wheels, springs and screws, until it was deposited at the far end with every minute portion of the motor ready to be assembled. And this goes on incessantly during the work hours. There is no break, no waiting for fresh supplies. All runs smoothly and with incredible rapidity. To the uninitiated eye it seems like magic.

From this section of the works the finished parts are at once transferred to other departments to be polished and assembled. The delicate process of assembling is almost entirely accomplished by girls and women, whose busy fingers are never still. They have all been specially trained in this branch and right deftly and daintily they perform their work.

A section which impressed us as strongly as anything we saw was the testing-room, where each completed motor had to be put through its facings, as it were. Gradations of speed have to be accurately determined, and as every bit of mechanism is standardized, each of the products has to run a stated number of records. After that comes a most important function—the test for silence. The motor which is absolutely noiseless is the ideal after which every manufacturer strives, and it is amazing how near perfection this object has been attained. The persons who perform the test are all abnormally acute of hearing and have been specially selected on that account. They listen with concentrated attention, and the very slightest buzz is at once detected, with the result that the offending motor is rejected. As in the past it has been a frequent occurrence for cheap motors to develop noise in running as soon as their pristine newness has worn off, it is good to see that these British makers pay a peculiar regard to the silence test.

Before we left that factory we learned some important facts which will doubtless surprise some of our readers. Each motor consists of 84 separate parts, without screws. If you include these the number mounts up to 189, and every one of them is turned out in the works, so you can understand why the tireless fingers of the assemblers appear to be so busy.

We will now proceed to what is undoubtedly the most important factor in the reproduction of sound—the reproducer or sound box, as it is most commonly called. Between the original type employed on the phonograph and that now used on the disc machine there exists a considerable difference, but that, after all, is only in detail, the principle being the same in both.

By the courtesy of
Messrs. J. E. Hough, Ltd.

A TYPICAL SOUND
BOX

The diaphragm, which is the true reproducer, may be made of various substances, of which we shall speak later. Anyone who examines a sound box will have a round flat surface presented to him, resembling, to a certain extent, the dial of a watch. That is the diaphragm, and it is the vibratory movement of that circular surface which causes the sound to be sent forth, in fact, you might compare it to the vocal chords of the machine.

The box itself is invariably of metal. Other substances such as wood and vulcanite have been experimented upon, but they have been found unsuitable, because, being softer, they absorb the sound. Metal, too, is more convenient for the exact fitting of the parts. The form of the case is almost always round. A square one with rounded corners has recently been seen, and is said to give good results, but that is altogether an exception. The case, which has a circular outlet in the centre, having been manufactured, the next step in the construction of a reproducer is the setting of the diaphragm. Two rubber rings, known as gaskets, are inserted round the inner edge of the box in such a manner as to grip the diaphragm tightly between them. Then comes the fixing of the stylus bar, which is a somewhat delicate process.

To the tyro we would explain' that the stylus bar is that little arm of steel—it may be of other metal but steel is the more frequently used—which may be seen advancing half-way across the face of the diaphragm. It will be observed that it does not touch the material from the side to the centre, but at the precise point in the middle of the circle it is attached to the diaphragm substance, having the end more or less bent round for that purpose. The function of the stylus bar is to impart the vibration to the diaphragm which has arisen from the needle running along the track of the record. To achieve this the butt of the stylus bar, if we may so call it, is mounted on a fulcrum or bridge where it receives a rocking motion from the record which is instantaneously communicated to the diaphragm at its centre, thus giving the necessary thrust and pull of vibration. Every sound box maker has a different system for fixing and adjusting the stylus bar upon its fulcrum with screws and springs, so that we cannot speak of a universal method. New types are being invented every day, but it will be hard to beat the Exhibition sound box of the Gramophone Company.[1]

The back of the case may be made of the same metal as the sides, or of aluminium or fibrous material, but

[1] A very competent authority, Mr. Louis Young, maintains that there is no need for a fulcrum or springs, and that the same result could be achieved if the stylus bar were soldered to the rim of the sound box. He gives as his reason that the waves are molecular disturbances which would carry through without these interventions.

great care must be taken that the plate is neither too thick nor too thin, else the correct tonal effects will be interfered with. There is a round opening in the backing to permit the sound to pass through when the box is attached to the gooseneck or tone arm. The size and weight of the sound box are rather important matters, because, in the first place, a heavy reproducer will cause much greater wear and tear to records than a

By the courtesy of the Gramophone Co., Ltd.

THE EXHIBITION SOUND BOX

light one, and, in the second, if it be too light it will probably fail to enter all the sinuosities of the track and on that account give forth an imperfect reproduction. In regard to size, it stands to reason that a large diaphragm will reproduce sounds of greater amplitude than one smaller, but it is said by experts that what is gained in volume is lost in fidelity, and that the big diaphragm does not give us the finer shades that have been recorded.

Concerning substances from which diaphragms have

been made, there is hardly anything of a hard, and at the same time elastic nature which has not been tried. Metals of various kinds, woods of all descriptions (including cork), ivory, xylonite, paper, cardboard, mica and glass, are among the most common of the materials which have been used, and certain fibrous compositions have also been employed, with, at least in one instance, considerable success. Of all that we have enumerated, however, there is none that can equal glass for both brilliance and completeness of reproduction. At one time it was much in use, but its brittleness and fragility have caused it to be discarded in favour of mica. It is still, however, largely in use for recording diaphragms, in which capacity it is not exposed to the rough treatment to which sound boxes are submitted by ignorant gramophonists. Mica, being of laminated structure, is apt to split, which is, of course, a drawback, but careful selection and examination of the portions to be employed will obviate such occurrences. Our friend Seymour, among his countless other experiments, introduced a diaphragm of baked carbon sheet, " with remarkable results," he says, " as to strength and fidelity of tone, but a certain deficiency in brilliancy was noticeable. Its greatest success was most conspicuous with records of large amplitude." He is convinced, he tells us, that an excellent field of research lies in the direction of malleable glass for diaphragm use. It is quite evident that the last word has not yet been spoken concerning sound boxes.

All the Gramophone Company's machines, and indeed almost all machines of quality are now provided with the gooseneck attachment which facilitates the changing of the needle. It is also claimed for it that it reduces any harshness that there may be in the record, but we are not altogether confident about that. However, there

5—(1466E)

can be no gainsaying that it serves its first-mentioned purpose well, and is a great convenience in use.

The tone arm for disc machines did not come into general use until about the year 1905. We believe the inventor to have been Jensen, but there are others who lay claim to the innovation and we will not discuss the matter. At all events, some time in the early years of the present century the Gramophone Company took out a patent for a tapered tone arm jointed to the horn or amplifier. The taper in this accessory gave a gradual increase in the circumference of the arm from the sound box to the joint where it met the horn, thus amplifying the sound the whole way, as we see in certain musical instruments of the band and orchestra. Previously the tone arm had been straight. In the early machines the record had borne the whole weight of both sound box and horn, but when the tone arm came in vogue the horn was supported by a rigid bracket firmly screwed to the cabinet and the tone arm swung free.

In 1906 the Gramophone Company brought an action against Messrs. C. and J. Ullmann, who were running the Odeon, for infringement of their tone arm patent. The case caused much excitement in the talking machine world, because at that time the contest between cylinder and disc was at its height. Counsel argued learnedly on both sides and experts were called as witnesses by each litigant, but the Gramophone Company lost the day, with the result that anyone who chose could use the tapered arm We fancy that nowadays, the only manufacturing companies that do not use it are the Columbia, who employ an arm fashioned at its curve in the shape of a cornet, and Pathé Frères and the Aeolian, their arms being straight

Tone arms are chiefly made of metal, aluminium being high in favour because of its lightness, but another of

Mr. Seymour's inventions has been the employment of a closely grained wood tube between the sound box and the second elbow. This, he maintains, is an improvement, and we see no reason to disagree with him after the change that has taken place by the substitution of the wood horn for the old-fashioned tin. The manufacture of tone arms is another of those industries which was mainly in the hands of the German, but several firms have recently added this to other kinds of metal work in the Midlands and are doing uncommonly well.[1]   .

The taste of the public seems now to run upon hornless machines of all sorts, and beautiful specimens of the cabinet maker's art are displayed on all sides, camouflaging the real instrument. Some of these disguised gramophones cost as much as two or three hundred pounds, and even more, the purchaser being mulcted to that extent, not because of the superior quality of the machine itself, but by reason of its appearance as an article of furniture. To our mind the principle of the concealed horn is an entire mistake. By the irrefragible law of acoustics the tendency of sound is to rise. What has now become the old-fashioned horn diffused the sound throughout the apartment. The concealed horn turns the sound down and it is emitted through an opening in the body of the cabinet, which may be closed or open. A frequent method is not to

[1] We have quite recently seen a square wood tone arm in connection with a hornless gramophone. It gives fairly good results, but is not yet on the market. Another type is made of hollowed beech, in two sections, smoothly polished inside and out. It has just been brought out and is known as the " All Wood " tone arm. Great difficulty was experienced by the inventor in getting the tapered bore round the angle, but success came to him at last, and the accessory promises to be of great service Used with a wooden amplifier all the disagreeable metallic sound will disappear.

have a horn at all but a sound chamber which is of any shape that the exigencies of space determine. If the space be square the sound will reverberate from side to side and become confused. Besides, being confined, the sound must necessarily be restricted. It cannot give the value in volume which was obtained from the open horn.

The best kind of open horn is, of course, that made of wood. It does away with the harsh, metallic sound

A TYPICAL TABLE GRAND MODEL OF
THE COLUMBIA GRAFONOLA

which the early trumpets invariably gave forth, and was in a great measure the cause of the prejudice which formerly existed against the instrument. With a good wood horn, and the best makes of other accessories, the gramophone is not an instrument to be ashamed of, and we see no reason why one should wish to hide his talking machine under another guise—a view shared, we know, by several manufacturers, who, however, have had to bow to the public demand for the cabinet type.

One of the most indispensable accessories of the gramophone is the needle. In the cylinder machine it is permanently affixed to the diaphragm in the form of a sapphire or diamond point, but in the case of the disc machine it is, except with phono-cut records, a separate entity. Its duty is to follow the sound waves which have been transformed into sinuosities in the bed of the track and transmit the vibrations to the sound box, where, as we have seen, these vibrations are reconverted into sound by the diaphragm and sent out through the tone arm and amplifier to the world at large. The needle, then, is the first link in the chain between the record and the human ear.

Many are the varieties of needles employed in the reproduction of sound, the most common of all being the short slip of steel wire sharpened to a point. These are now manufactured in their thousands of millions and are sold in boxes containing a hundred. Redditch, which is the centre of the sewing needle and fish-hook industry, took up the gramophone needle business as soon as the makers found there was a demand for these small wares, and has thus added considerably to its prosperity. Sheffield, too, has done well out of them, and there are small factories in other parts of the country.

Every record manufacturing company now send out their own needles, but in the days when the Berliner disc was first introduced to this country the purchaser of a machine had to be content with a single, solitary needle to play all records of the new class. One of the earliest gramophone users in the United Kingdom has told us that in the year 1893 he bought a Berliner " grammaphon," as the word was then spelt, and along with it received the precious steel needle. This he kept for *three years*, sharpening it occasionally on emery cloth.

When it defied sharpening he took to sewing needles. What the state of that gentleman's records must have been we dread to think.

When the Gramophone Company began to trade in disc machines in this country at the commencement of this century, they sold their needles separately, but they were all of one class, loud toned and giving a coarse reproduction. Soon afterwards it was discovered that a great deal depended upon the needle in tone-value, in true verisimilitude and in volume. Experiments were made and different kinds of the steel needle were manufactured, loud toned, soft toned, medium toned, and so forth Disc enthusiasts changed their needles for each class of record, a certain needle for voice reproduction, another for instrumental, and still another for bands and orchestras Some went as far as to use special needles for each kind of voice, soprano, contralto, tenor and bass, and also for solo instruments, violin, piano, etc. We are told that a few *dilletanti* do so regularly now and doubtless they are on the right side.

The great drawback to the steel needle is that it should never be used more than once. Some benighted people, seeing directions to that effect upon the box, imagine it to be a dodge to sell more needles, but they were never more mistaken in their lives If they desire to keep their records from wearing out rapidly it is essential that the needle should be changed with every disc placed upon the turntable. The record is made of an exceedingly hard, though somewhat brittle, material. The track upon the surface, if extended in a straight line, would measure several hundred feet. The point has to traverse the whole of that distance, and must necessarily become worn in doing so. If it were worn evenly it would not so much matter, but the mischief

of it is that it is not. . As the record revolves the needle
is pressed inwardly against the side of the groove, and
the point is ground flat where the pressure takes place.
As it gradually nears the centre of the disc the needle
becomes more upright and the pressure is not so great,
but in assuming its new position it presents an edge to
the side of the track which cuts into the substance,

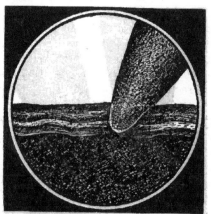

By the courtesy of Messrs. J. E. Hough, Ltd.

UNUSED CHROMIC NEEDLE RUNNING IN GROOVE

(Microscopically enlarged by James Scott)

hard though it be. When this needle is used again and
starts at the outside of the record it will be at a slightly
different angle, and the cutting process will begin
immediately. There was a splendid article upon this
subject in the *Talking Machine News* some time ago
by Mr. James Scott, the well-known microscopist, with
greatly magnified drawings of the damage done as seen
under the microscope. If every gramophone user were
to read that article and examine those illustrations he

would never submit a record to the same needle a second time.

In the year 1908 a Mr. Frederick Durize Hall, of Chicago, took out a patent for what he called a " fibre " needle, the material of which it is made being a fibrous vegetable substance, " preferably bamboo." This " preferably bamboo," we suppose, means that the patent

By the courtesy of Messrs J. E. Hough, Ltd.

NEEDLES SHOWING WEAR BY CONTACT WITH RECORD

should cover all types of fibre needles, but we don't think that it would. Anyhow, bamboo is the " vegetable substance " of which all these styli are formed, and for the last nine or ten years a miniature war has been waged between the supporters of the old-fashioned steel needle and the followers of the new cult. There can be no doubt that the army of the latter is increasing. Recruits are coming in every day and the fibre has gained a firm footing in the gramophone world. The shape of this needle is triangular and the point is formed

by a slanting cross section so that one of the angles fits
into the groove of the record.   In using this fibre
stylus it is necessary to have a triangular hole cut,
instead of the usual round one, in the needle socket of
the sound box, because the little screw of the holder will
not give a sufficiently firm grip.   Having this done,
however, spoils the holder for future use with the steel
needle.   To obviate this disadvantage Mr. Daws Clarke,
of Manchester, has patented an ingenious little fitment,
known as the Needle Tension Attachment, by which
either the steel or the fibre needle may be rendered
perfectly rigid.   This invention gives an improved tone
to reproduction no matter which kind of needle is
used.   There is also another accessory we have seen,
with a short round shank to fit in the round needle
hole, and a triangular cutting at the other end for the
fibre.

To those who prefer a soft and even reproduction,
with a diminution of surface scratch, to the loud, and
sometimes strident, tones of the steel needle, the fibre
is certainly to be recommended, but there is an imper-
fection in it that cannot be disguised.   It will not last
more than one side of the record through without
re-sharpening, and we have found it fail to play a twelve
inch record satisfactorily to the end, which is most
annoying.   Several little implements have been brought
out to effect the repointing, the best of which we consider
to be the Wade, a pliers like tool which is so set that
a blade snips off the point at the correct angle.

While on the subject of the fibre needle we may
mention that not long ago we had some ordinary hedge-
row thorns sent to us as samples by a gentleman who is
the secretary of one of our most prosperous talking
machine societies and a great enthusiast.   These had been
cut, trimmed and dried, and though their appearance

might have been a little crude they gave forth a reproduction almost as good as the vaunted fibre needle. Under these circumstances there is no reason why every gramophonist should not become his own needle provider.

There is another natural needle of which we have heard excellent accounts, but it belongs to the animal and not the vegetable kingdom. That is the hedgehog spine. We have never listened to a record played by this singular stylus, but we were in conversation with a gentleman not long ago who had been spending a holiday in Devonshire and had heard many reproductions by means of these sharp-pointed quills. His report of them is entirely favourable He tells us that he believes them to be better than the fibre needle and that the reproduction lasts longer.

To return to the steel needle, there is a variant of it in the spear-point, of which there are a good many varieties. The advantage of this is that it may be used in three or four different ways. Having played a record through with the flat of the spear head at right angles to the groove you turn it round and get the other side to work. That finished, by a half turn you get the flanges parallel with the track, and you can repeat the operation for the remaining side It is said that by these four turns the two double-sided records which they cover do not suffer, but we " ha'e oor doots."

Besides the sapphire and diamond tipped styli used for phono-cut records which are permanently attached to the sound box, there was put upon the market some years ago a diamond pointed needle shaped not unlike a very small peg-top with a thin shank to fit into the ordinary holder, and we understand a needle of the same description with a glass point was also tried, but the difficulty and expense of manufacture proved too great, though the points were practically everlasting.

Tungsten wire fitted into a nickel sheath is the latest thing for the needle-cut disc.   The first of these that we saw came to us all the way from Chile, some two or three years ago, but we were not greatly impressed by it. Since then the Gramophone Company have brought out a similar stylus, under the name of the Tungstyle Needle, but in our opinion it will not be a success.   The reproduction by it is thin and hard like the needle itself, and though it is guaranteed to play something like a hundred and fifty records without the necessity of changing, we don't believe it will ever take the place of a good soft steel point. Tungsten, of course, is ever so much harder than steel, and its wearable quality is therefore vastly superior, but there the advantage of the tungstyle stops.   There are hard steel needles issued by various manufacturers which will play up to ten records without wear, but we never heard any of these that we cared for.   The tone has always been too metallic.   The Chromic needle, issued by J. E. Hough, Ltd , is, however, a good one.   It is of a golden hue and will play its ten records without fail.   As good a needle as we know is the Ideal belonging to the Columbia Company, and this we most frequently use for the sample records submitted to us for review, this being a soft-tone (*piano*), though we believe the same company's loud-tone (*forte*) " Superbe " needle is most popular generally.

The war between the fibre and the steel needle still goes on, and we daresay will continue to go on till some new material is discovered combining the good qualities of both.   Until then we shall remain strictly neutral.

CHAPTER VI

HOW GRAMOPHONE RECORDS ARE MADE

ONCE upon a time we had our voice recorded upon a disc, so that we can tell from personal experience what the initiatory process is like. It was about ten years ago and we had perpetrated what in our secret soul we imagined to be a poem. We daresay it was poor stuff, but, as the subject was topical, the manager of a certain company believed it might have an ephemeral sale, which would pay for the production and a bit more, so we were persuaded to have it embalmed in shellac. As a matter of fact the record was a dead failure, not from the recording point of view, but because it was actually too late for the market. The presumably wretched verses, we may tell you, were recited not sung.

Having ascended an interminable number of stairs we found ourselves in an absolutely bare apartment save for a single music stand. A tall, stout young gentleman—he is now one of the greatest recording experts in the world—came to us and in an affable manner announced that everything was ready. He pointed to a long trumpet-like tube which projected from the wall and directed us to take up our position in front of it with our mouth about 6 ins. from the opening. " When the light shows," he said " you can fire away." Then he left us alone. It was desperately uncanny, but we braced ourselves for the inevitable.

Presently the light flashed, and we spouted for all we were worth to an unseen audience. Half-way through we made a slip and immediately the light signalled.

The young gentleman spoke from the other side of the wall. " It's a pity," he remarked; " you were doing very well, but I've got another blank."

After a time the light flashed once more and we started from the beginning as before. Straight through we went to the end without a falter, and then there came from beyond the partition the order to wait a minute. We waited till all at once there broke upon our ear from the other end of the horn an unknown voice repeating the rhymes we had previously uttered on the spoiled record. It was most curious, but it did not sound to ourselves as our own voice. Robert Burns says, " Oh, wad some power the giftie gi'e us to see oorsel's as ithers see us," but the gramophone has now brought to us the power of hearing ourselves as others hear us, and the result is not in the least like that which we had imagined. We are deceived by our own tones. Our friends hear them in quite a different key from that in which we believe them to be uttered ; at least, that was our first impression on listening to them. Afterwards, when we became accustomed to the record, the strange feeling wore off.

For a few minutes we stood in the bare room waiting for further developments, and then the recorder returned to us. In his open hands he carried the wax wherein was deposited our poem with all its imperfections.

" I believe I've got you all right," he said, and we put on our glasses and gazed upon the thing he held. There was nothing to be seen except the crowded grooves upon the substance he displayed to us. We intimated that we were satisfied, and shaking hands with the man who had taken irrevocable possession of our voice, we descended the long, long stairs and so to the busy street.

A few days afterwards catastrophe befell. A wire called us back to the recording room. In the process of

manufacture the wax master had been damaged, and
the whole operation of recording had to be repeated.
This delayed the issue of the disc and the market
was lost.   For that reason our poem has not gone down
to posterity, and we remain a " mute inglorious Milton."

All recordings, however, are not performed in the

SIR HENRY J. WOOD CONDUCTING THE NEW QUEEN'S
HALL ORCHESTRA FOR A COLUMBIA RECORD

simple fashion we have described.   There are the vocal
records of duets, trios, quartettes and choruses to be
made, with their accompaniments.   Then we have
bands and orchestras.   All the great military bands,
Grenadiers, Coldstreams, Scots Guards, Irish Guards
and Welsh Guards are constantly being recorded, and
to pack these big organizations into a recording room
requires a good deal of ingenuity.   The performers,
too, must be placed in such positions that no single

instrument must predominate, the just ensemble must be preserved. Experience has taught how this is to be adjusted, and the conductor who has had a good knowledge of the recording room will generally settle his men down or up without much difficulty.

When a large body of musicians have to make a record there are often three or four recording horns employed, converging on a point in the partition for the purpose of collecting the sound waves and concentrating them upon the diaphragm. It will at once be perceived that in this way a fuller reproduction can be accomplished.

There are certain musical instruments which have proved very baffling to the recorder. For many years the violin and the piano were both enormous stumbling blocks. Indeed, it is only quite recently that the latter has been brought into subjection. Formerly the notes of a piano, as heard on the talking machine, seemed to emanate from a banjo, but now, by dint of careful experiment and enlarged experience, the recording expert has brought the reproduction as close to perfection as the gramophone up to the present time can bring it. We listened a few weeks ago to a record from which was reproduced a piece by Saint Saëns, played by the great French pianist, M. Alfred Cortot, in which the exact tones of a grand piano were given without the slightest difference from the instrument, save for the inevitable surface scratch. It is now the same with the violin.

In November, 1920, there arrived in this country from America eight records by that amazing Russian youth, Jascha Heifetz. A party of the greatest musicians and critics in this country was called together at the Piccadilly Hotel to hear them. Those experts were astounded at the marvellous technique of the young executant—he was then only nineteen—so much so, indeed, that one of the most noted composers of England dubbed him " the modern Paganini."   Six months later Heifetz himself reached London to give four performances in as many weeks at the Queen's Hall.   At the first of these there was a great gathering of the *cognoscenti*. Next morning the worst one of our leading dailies could find to say against the youthful virtuoso was that he played exactly like his records.   It was intended for disparagement, but could a greater tribute have been paid to the gramophone ?   Incidentally we may mention that, before Heifetz set his foot on British soil, the Gramophone Company, of Hayes, Middlesex—the great concern which manufactures and issues the famous " His Master's Voice " discs—had sold no fewer than 70,000 of his records ! This is an extraordinary ·fact, and illustrates very clearly the vast development of the talking machine industry in this country within recent years.

To get behind the scenes of the recording room, that is, into the *sanctum sanctorum* of the recorder, is a very difficult matter, for the secrets there are most jealously guarded.   It has been our privilege, however, to be admitted into one of these inner sanctuaries, and, without giving away any of the hidden technicalities of the process we witnessed, for each recorder has his own individual methods, we can give a general description which will not reveal more than is necessary.

On stepping into the private domain of the recording expert we were at once sensible of a considerable rise in the temperature.   We read in a newspaper the other day that this access of heat is perceptible in the outer room, but we cannot say that, on the occasion of our first visit, when we made the record of which we have spoken, we experienced the slightest change. However, we dare say, if the exterior recording room be crowded with a band, orchestra, or full chorus the atmosphere would become somewhat stifling. There is no necessity for the public room, as we may call it, to be artificially heated, but it is different with the inner chamber. There the temperature must be maintained at a certain height because the wax of the blanks has to be of the requisite consistency for the recording needle to run smoothly. These blanks are kept in warmed cupboards around the room, and when the operator is at work they must be in perfect condition. Several of them may be spoiled in the making of a record, when they have afterwards to be submitted to a process of " shaving " by a special instrument invented for the purpose.

Although we play on the talking machine with one sound box for all manner of records, in the cutting of the blank many different sound boxes are used. Thus the recorder will employ one for soprano, another for contralto, and so on, varying his reproducers as experience has taught him. It is wonderful what a variety are necessary. For instance, a sound box which will make a perfect reproduction of a violin solo will be of no use in recording a string quartette, so one can imagine the years of close study and intense application which the expert must go through before he is qualified to make a record of a Caruso or a Heifetz. There are not many highly skilled recorders, and it is not needful that there should be, for the record manufacturers in this country are few and far between ; but when once a manufacturing firm has found an expert who is thoroughly capable it is very loth to let him go, so that most of these truly scientific gentlemen may reckon upon high salaries and continuous service.

In making a record it is absolutely incumbent upon the recording machine being completely stable, for the

6—(1466E)

slightest vibration of the stylus other than that imparted by the diaphragm will render the reproduction worthless. Therefore, not only must the turntable on which the blank is imposed run freely and steadily, but the supports must be immovable, so that no tremor can reach the wax while the stylus is doing its work. The motive power varies in different recording rooms. Some prefer an electric motor, while others use weight-driven mechanism like those of the old-fashioned grandfather's clocks, but heavier. The latter was the system in vogue with the firm whose room we were allowed to inspect. They claim that the movement is steadier, though even then, delicately balanced governors are adjusted to ensure invariability.

We have previously mentioned that the recording diaphragm is almost always of glass, as it is the substance most amenable to the action of the sound waves. A lever attachment fits it to the cutting point, which is in nearly every case a jewel that has been most carefully treated for the purpose of performing its work with the utmost exactitude.

The wax blank having been selected, dusted to remove every particle of foreign matter and placed upon the turntable, the recorder gives the signal and the pianist in the next room begins the symphony to a song. The artist follows with the air and all the time the blank is spinning with the turntable We watch it with a sort of fascination. Thin threads of composition curl up from the jewel point and are blown off as they rise, till presently the song is finished, and the vacant space on the wax has become covered with the grooves that are so familar to us on the finished record

On the day we visited the company's premises the artist who was engaged was a well-known lady singer,

who is a great favourite among gramophone users.   She
has made many records and is quite accustomed to the
horn, yet the expert would not allow the first to pass.
He put it through on the wax, but it would not satisfy
him, and it was not until he had taken the third or fourth
of the same song, that he gave a kind of grumbling
consent to let it go.   You see, these gentlemen are so
very exacting.

When, at last, he was to a certain extent pleased, he
took up the wax, went over it carefully with a camel's
hair brush and packed it in a box with cotton wool.
It was ready to be dispatched to the factory.

That was the whole of our recording room experience,
but it was only the beginning of the adventures of the
disc.   It had still to go through several processes before
it emerged from the factory a fully developed record.
Some of these we have attempted to explain in our chapter on the Disc Machine, but there will be no harm in
laying the whole process before our readers succinctly
and clearly before we pass on to other matters.

As soon as the wax record, which is called the master,
arrives at the factory it is plunged into the electrotyping
bath which deposits on its surface a copper coating
that enters into every twist and wriggle made by the
recording needle within the grooves.   These, of course,
represent the sound waves passed on by the vibrations
of the diaphragm.   When this coating is sufficiently
thick it is removed and brings with it the exact impression of the wax reversed.   This forms a complete mould
and might be used as such, as, indeed, it was at one
time, but so many accidents by breakage and such
like took place that nowadays the companies run no
risks.   Other wax impressions are made from it which
in their turn are electrotyped, so that several matrices
are formed, which are then nickel-plated, polished and

receive a strong backing of heavy steel as a support. They are then ready for the presses. Before going into that, however, we may as well tell you about the substance that is pressed into the moulds.

Recently there has been a good deal of grumbling about the advanced prices of records, and some of the manufacturing companies have explained that the chief contributing cause of this has been the enormously increased cost of shellac. Numbers of the public wanted to know what shellac had to do with it, being completely unaware that shellac is the principal ingredient in the manufacture of disc records. Many believed that the discs, with their beautifully polished surfaces, were made of vulcanite. In fact, a friend of ours only the other day was so convinced of this that he offered to lay pretty heavy odds that they were. It was a difficult matter to undeceive him, and not until we produced a book on the subject would he admit that he was wrong. The actual ingredients are shellac, the mineral barytes, rotten stone, flock (made from rags) and lamp-black. Different companies use these components in varying quantities, but if the records be analysed they will all be found to consist of each of these substances. They are ground together and then passed through heated rollers which melt the shellac, with the result that the whole becomes a soft black paste which hardens when cold, and is then broken up into square pieces.

When the discs pass into the pressing room the steel backing is laid upon a heated table with the mould upwards, and the label of the record is placed face downwards against the centre of the mould. A few pieces of the hard black preparation are then heated until they soften, when they are transferred to the warm disc. If a single-sided record be desired a steel plate of the size of the under disc is placed on the top, but if the record is to be double-faced, another mould is placed face downwards over the black material, with the label between. The pair are then moved into a powerful hydraulic press and the black composition is flattened out to the thickness of the record, working itself into every groove and infinitesimal sinuosity by the pressure placed upon it. When it cools it is quite hard and only requires trimming, which is done by placing the record between two revolving discs and applying sandpaper to the whirling edge. The labels have adhered to the centre of the record by reason of the sticky nature of the shellac, and the records are then carried off to the examiner who tests them. The inferior ones are rejected and those which are passed are placed in the envelopes for the market.

CHAPTER VII

IN England at the present time there are four companies manufacturing the higher priced records. Of these The Gramophone Company, Ltd., undoubtedly holds the field. The history of this extensive concern has already been referred to cursorily in a previous chapter, but we would like to lay before the reader a more comprehensive chronicle of its origin and rise.

Like most of the other large firms engaged in the industry The Gramophone Company began its career in America. As previously stated, Berliner was the man who gave the term " gramophone " to his invention of a disc machine, though he never claimed an exclusive right thereto. In 1896 or 1897 Berliner sold his English patent rights, including, it is said, his rights in respect of certain patented improvements, to a private firm calling itself The Gramophone Company, taking its name from the instrument. In 1899 this concern transferred its business to a company incorporated under the style of The Gramophone Company, Limited, the object of which, as defined by its Memorandum of Association, embraced, *inter alia*, the manufacture and sale of gramophones and phonographs and gramophone discs and phonograph cylinders. The last mentioned firm continued to sell machines and discs made under Berliner's patent until the following year, when it parted with its business to a company with a larger capital. This new concern had about the same time acquired an interest in typewriters, and was incorporated as The Gramophone and Typewriter Company, Limited.

72

The same year the Tainter-Bell patent expired, and the graving method being considered superior to etching, the company abandoned the latter process and adopted the former, continuing, however, to use the name of gramophone. There was nothing wrong in that, for the essence of the Berliner system was the sinuous line of even depth and the word " gramophone " had come to denote a disc talking machine, as opposed to the phonograph and graphophone which were at that time operated by cylinders.

The Gramophone and Typewriter Company established a branch in England almost as soon as it was inaugurated, with Mr. Barry Owen as its representative, and some time afterwards dropped the typewriter section of the business, reverting to the old title of The Gramophone Company, Ltd. They had their offices in Maiden Lane, Covent Garden, and so rapid was the growth of this British branch that a company was formed with a share capital of £600,000, the ordinary shares in the first instance being offered to the trade. Thereupon they removed to the City Road where they remained in full swing until the extensive works at Hayes, Middlesex, which were opened in 1907, were ready to receive the army of workers of every description attached to the firm. This enormous factory has been enlarged and developed since that date until it now covers twenty-three acres of ground.

Ever since the expiry of Berliner's 1887 patent The Gramophone Company had arrogated to itself the sole right to the term " gramophone." In its dealings with the trade it had consistently claimed monopoly rights in the word as denoting goods of its own manufacture only, and by warning circulars, legal proceedings and threats of legal proceedings, had done its best to support its exclusive claims. Other manufacturers refrained from describing their instruments as gramophones from the dread of infringing the alleged rights of the company. The gigantic bubble, however, was destined to be pricked.

In the year 1910 the company applied for power to register the term " gramophone " as applicable solely to the wares manufactured and dealt in by them. The most memorable case ever heard of in the talking machine world of this country ensued. It came before Mr. Justice Parker and lasted four days. Experts, legal and otherwise, were called, examined and cross-examined. The court was crammed with all the leading lights of the trade, who were there either as witnesses or as spectators. At length judgment was pronounced Power was refused, and the word " gramophone " became the property of anyone who had a disc machine to sell. A verbatim note of the whole proceedings was taken at the time by the *Talking Machine News*, and was published the morning after judgment was delivered. It was the only paper that printed the case *in extenso*.

In legal matters The Gramophone Company have been rather unfortunate, for previous to the case we have spoken of they lost one over the Gibson tapering tone arm in 1906. This was an invention for which they claimed sole rights. These were disputed and the action went against them. Nevertheless, if they have been unlucky in the courts it cannot be denied they have been marvellously successful in business. Before the war there were subsidiary companies in various capitals of Europe, and they were connected with the great Victor Company of America, which has now a large controlling interest in the concern. The Zonophone Company, too, has been absorbed by this firm.

During the war a portion of the huge factory at

Hayes, the foundation-stone of which, by the way, was laid by Madame Tetrazzini, was given over to the manufacture of munitions. It is believed that The Gramophone Company was the first industrial concern, not normally engaged on Government contracts, to convert their plant. Within ten days of the declaration of war, the output of certain essential fuse parts was commenced. These required extraordinary accuracy and the mechanism at command of the company enabled them to make a beginning almost at once.

Of the artists exclusively engaged to make the famous " His Master's Voice " records for the company we shall speak later, and in the chapter devoted to the " Talking Machine as a Teacher " we shall have something to say of the firm's efforts in that direction.

In 1899 The Columbia Phonograph Company was established in Washington, U.S.A., thus it may be said to be among the very earliest of the concerns to enter the industry, and it has been one of the most successful. As early as 1887, however, the parent company of the Columbia, and literally the pioneers in the industry, had put machines and cylinders on the market under licence from Bell and Tainter. Being unable to carry out some of their contracts, the American Company made arrangements with several others in the various States to act as sales-agents, while the original company limited their efforts to the manufacturing side. The Columbia Company secured one of these sales-agencies, and were restricted by agreement to the three States of Columbia, Delaware and Maryland. This restriction did not last long, however, for the prosperity of the Columbia was such that presently it ousted all the other agencies, extending its business throughout the whole of the United States. Not content with that, it opened branches all over the world and subsequently swallowed up the American Graphophone Company itself. Here it may be noted that, as we fancy we have mentioned before, it was T. H. Macdonald, of the Graphophone Company, who perfected the spring motor. Up till then electricity had been used for the driving power, but with the clockwork mechanism methods were simplified and the cost of machines considerably cheapened.

When the Columbia Company removed their chief offices from Washington to New York, Mr. Frank Dorian was placed in charge as general manager. This move occasioned a vast expansion of trade and Mr. Dorian was sent to Paris to superintend the establishment of the European connection. His energy proved invaluable. Rapid strides were made in Paris and a branch was soon opened in Berlin. The following year the London business was reorganized and its headquarters formed in a five storey building in Oxford Street This was made the controlling centre for Europe, and Columbia was flourishing like the green bay tree, Later their swiftly developing progress warranted a removal to larger premises in Great Eastern Street, closer to the seat of the British trade which lies in that neighbourhood. At that time, of course, their records were all cylinders, but they were doing admirable work. It was about this time that they contrived to obtain a record of the voice of Pope Leo XIII, a circumstance which we have already noted. It was issued almost on the very day of the venerable Pontiff's death, and so made a great sensation in Catholic circles. They also secured some valuable cylinders of famous singers of the time, and set a fashion later developed by the discs of the Gramophone Company.

Finding that, in England, the disc was superseding the cylinder, the Columbia built a factory at

Wandsworth and started manufacturing lateral cut records. It was an excellent step on their part, for they got hold of some of the best voices and instrumentalists in the kingdom and their productions had a great vogue. This company has played a conspicuous part in the fortunes of the industry here, doing excellent pioneer work in various directions, and aiming to elevate the public taste in gramophone music.

With the advent of Mr. Louis Sterling as European manager of the company fresh life was imparted into the business, and their instruments, the celebrated Grafonolas, have a great sale, while the records find purchasers by the million. The Regal, a cheaper record, is also issued by them and is much appreciated by gramophone users whose purses are not so well filled as those of the purchasers of the higher grade Columbia.

Pathé Frères, who had been doing a very large continental trade, came into the English market in 1902. By the exercise of a little ingenuity, aided by Mr. J. E. Hough, they had previously circumvented the Edison embargo No sooner, however, were they free to export their goods from France to England than they began to do an extensive trade with us. The Pathé discs are phono-cut, i.e. they are of the hill and dale variety invented by Edison, and therefore require to be played with a special needle. To this end the firm supplies a sound box of its own with a permanent attachment of a ball-pointed sapphire. Quite recently it has brought out a reproducer which by a simple contrivance permits of a steel needle to be used for the lateral cut disc as well.

In the early days Pathé records were played from the centre outward to the periphery of the disc, but since the company erected a British factory on this side the Channel they have reversed their old system and the record is now played in the same manner as other discs. Those old discs were splendid fellows, nearly 14 ins. across and embodied the voices of many of the best continental artists.   The firm actually prevailed upon Sara Bernhardt to record her incomparable tones, and in the years to come that disc ought to be worth much more than its weight in gold.   The records are now somewhat reduced in size, conforming more to the width of ordinary makes, but the best of them at the present time are the most expensive on sale in England. It is worthy of mention that Pathé Frères were the first to introduce the language-teaching record, and it is quite possible that they may revert to this very useful method of instruction now that there is a demand for easy systems of learning foreign tongues.[1]

Besides building a factory here in England, Messrs. Pathé have established a large business in America, which we understand is extremely prosperous.   M. Jacques Pathé is at the head of affairs in London, and is a shrewd and competent director.   He fought in the war for his country and received high commendation for his service.   Although it has nothing to do with this little book it may not be out of place to state that Pathé Frères are a firm with very extensive interests in the kinematograph world.   The House of Pathé, with its defiant chanticleer as a trade-mark has branches in every corner of the civilized globe, and its machines and discs are familiar to everyone who has the slightest knowledge of the reproduction of sound.

The Aeolian Company of America first came into notice as the manufacturers of player-pianos and

---

[1] Since the above was written, Pathé Frères have brought out a needle-cut disc, the Actuelle, which seems to be doing fairly well.

instruments of that *genre*. With untold capital behind them they forged ahead with remarkable vigour. A fine hall, with magnificent show-rooms and business premises, was erected on an advantageous site in New York, and as if by magic the great corporation bounded into the forefront of the musical manufacturing world. But this was not achieved without deep thought and careful planning. For a long time there had been active brains at work, considering, devising, scheming, and not until every action of the future had been thoroughly weighed and balanced was a move made. As soon as the company felt itself to be on a sound and solid basis it mentally bridged the Atlantic and set up an English house in Bond Street, London. The Aeolian Hall on this side, with its high-class concerts and musical entertainments, is now one of the most popular features of the West End, and the Aeolian Orchestra, a specially selected body of musicians, is second to none in the kingdom. The spirit of enterprise pervaded the minds of all those who were in any way connected with the firm, and it was this spirit that brought forth the Aeolian-Vocalion, the talking machine which is the company's special product.

We are told that, in the late summer of 1912, there arrived in London a Mr. F. J. Empson, a resident of Sydney, Australia. He brought with him a gramophone in which was embodied a wonderful patented device for controlling musical effects. This, in the opinion of its inventor, added so immeasurably to the musical value and charm of the instrument that he thought he had but to show it to manufacturers to secure its immediate adoption. As has been the fate of so many geniuses, mechanical and otherwise, since the world began, Mr. Empson found it impossible to gain a satisfactory audience with those whom he approached. Discouraged and depressed he purchased his passage home and was on the point of sailing, when he accidentally encountered a friend to whom he related his disappointing experiences. This friend was well acquainted with the officials of the Aeolian Company's London house, and earnestly advised the poor, disheartened inventor to make one more attempt to have his contrivance exploited. He told him of the company and directed him to their offices.

With just one faint ray of hope illuminating the darkness of his mind, the inventor made his way to Bond Street. For the first time since his arrival in England the reception that he met with was satisfactory. The Aeolian officials were so impressed with the value of the new feature that they took an option on the patents, and instead of returning to Australia, he and his instrument were immediately shipped across to the head offices of the company in New York. There the directors and experts at once grasped the possibilities of the invention. Without delay they had the patents investigated, and on finding them sound and inclusive, closed with the inventor on a mutually satisfactory basis. Thus was the Aeolian-Vocalion, with its Graduola attachment, launched upon the world.

Apart from the advance made by the company in the style of their machines and the accuracy of reproduction of all records submitted to the test of the turntable, the Aeolian-Vocalion itself was voiceless, which means the firm manufactured no records of their own That was to be a big consideration for the future. In the meantime the energies of the concern were concentrated upon the Graduola. This device obviated the use of different toned needles, the muting of horns, the opening and closing of shutters, and all the various methods which had been adopted of altering the tone of the gramophone to suit the ear of the listener. It gave into the hands of the operator a perfect means of controlling the reproduction of the record. Modulation of the voice of a singer could be governed at the will of the gramophone user, and in that way the listener could guide to his ear inflexions and variations which were more agreeable to him than the actual recording.

It may be said that this principle is altogether wrong, and that if you choose to vary the conception of the vocalist you do not get the true value of the voice. This is undoubtedly quite right, but it very often happens that the idea of the listener is at variance with the idea of the singer. We know many persons who have no liking for the forceful tones of Caruso, but by the use of the Gráduola these may be so subdued that their beauty can be acknowledged and appreciated. The musical instinct of the listener imperceptibly directs him while he holds the little attachment in his hands.

The simple contrivance of Mr. Empson, like many other inventions, was merely the adaptation of a known fact to a new outlet. Everybody knows that air carries sound and that if the current be reversed the sound becomes fainter. Therein lies the secret of the Graduola. A slender, flexible tube connects the gramophone with the operator. At the end in the fingers of the manipulator is a valve which he pushes in or retracts according to his personal desire. Thus the sound given forth from the machine is regulated at the will of the performer. He, or she, can therefore listen to the record in the manner desired. It is as simple as A, B, C, but it had never been applied to the talking machine before the Aeolian-Vocalion made their arrangement with the inventor.

We have spoken of the Aeolian-Vocalion being

voiceless, inasmuch as the company produced no records, but that deficiency has, happily for all gramophone enthusiasts, been adequately made good. After more than two years of unremitting experiment the company have placed upon the market records which will hold their own, if not surpass, any that have previously been brought before the public. To our knowledge they have scrapped thousands which they did not consider up to the mark, and from their well equipped factory at Hayes, nothing but the very best are issued. They have secured good artists, although the field has been somewhat restricted in consequence of other companies having enrolled the greatest of vocalists and instrumentalists, yet they have made a splendid start and we feel certain that, as time goes on, they will hold one of the most exalted positions in the talking machine world.

Of cheap records one of the most popular of all is the Winner of J. E. Hough, Ltd., their annual output amounting on an average to 6,000,000, the present price being 2s. 6d. This go-ahead concern has now produced a higher priced record, the Velvet Faced (V.F.) in two sizes, 12 in. and 10 in., at 5s. 6d. and 3s. 6d. These are lovely discs with very little scratch.

The Zonophone, which belongs, as we have already stated, to the Gramophone Company, is a wonderful record at 3s., celebrities such as Sir Harry Lauder and a few others being a shilling dearer. Regal are the property of the Columbia Company and are well worth the 2s. 6d. charged for them. The Coliseum, Scala, Popular and Guardsman records are also of the cheap variety.

Since writing of the Edison disc in a previous chapter we have heard that these records are being imported into this country in quantities and that they·are much better than the first arrivals. Let us hope that this may be so, for those we listened to when first they made their appearance were atrocious. Edison has his idolaters—we are not of them.

An important phase, worth mentioning here, is that of the commercial phonograph, the most popular of which is the " Dictaphone," manufactured by the Columbia Graphophone Co., Ltd. The " Dictaphone " is a phonograph used by business men for direct dictation, dispensing with the shorthand writer, the stenographer transcribing from the cylinder, which repeats what has been recorded. It is a modern time-saving device and its success is such that most shipping and railway companies, banks, and large commercial houses equip every department, some of them having forty or more " Dictaphones " installed in this way. This, curiously enough, is the only form in which the one-time universal cylinder record exists—the disc proving unwieldy for this purpose.

CHAPTER VIII

ARTISTS WHO MAKE RECORDS

IN the very early days of the phonograph it was *really* a talking machine, for the first records of the human voice ever made were of speaking, not of singing. The congratulatory speech, or rather, message, of Mr. Gladstone to Edison on the success of the latter's great achievement was the kind of thing which did duty over and over again. It was unscrupulously imitated when the first cylinders became worn out, as they very rapidly did in those days before a hardening process was invented. Other great men were pressed into the service, and in quite recent years statesmen of the present day have been induced to make speeches into the recording horn.

At first, however, it was difficult to get singers of note to record their voices. Sir Landon Ronald, the Principal of the Guildhall School of Music, who was an early enthusiast on behalf of the gramophone, has told in an interview of the trouble he had to get over the scruples of Ben Davies, our great English tenor. Davies laughed at the bare idea of singing into a tin trumpet, but at length Mr. Ronald, as he then was, prevailed upon him to make the experiment, and accompanied him to the recording room of the Gramophone Company. Treating the matter more as a joke than anything else, notwithstanding the fact that the fee was a substantial one, the brilliant singer took up his position in front of the horn and gave forth to the world at large one of his favourite ballads. If we mistake not, the song was " My Pretty Jane," and when the famous vocalist heard it presently come back to him through the horn

84

he was electrified. That was many years ago, but
Mr. Davies, well over sixty years of age, is still making
records for the talking machine, in fact, he is on the
exclusive list for the Columbia Company, and his

By the courtesy of the Gramophone Co., Ltd.

MADAME ADELINA PATTI

beautiful voice, despite the lapse of time, is as clear as
a bell.

The immortal *diva*, Adelina Patti, for a long period
set her lovely face dead against all temptations of the
record, and it was not until her final retirement from the
operatic stage that she consented to submit her marvellous notes to the judgment of posterity. It was in 1905
that she chanced to hear some remarkable records by
Caruso. She was then sixty-two and living privately
with her husband at Craig-y-Nos, her charming castle
in Wales. Though she had been frequently urged in

the past to allow her voice to be impressed upon a disc she had consistently declined. The Caruso records, however, wrought a change in her. Suddenly, of her own accord, she sent to the Gramophone Company asking for arrangements to be made to have her voice recorded. The officials of the company were astonished, for they were well aware of her aversion to the talking machine, but they at once hastened to take advantage of her change of mind, lest, with a lady's privilege, she might change it again. The highly skilled recording expert of the firm, with assistants and musicians for the accompaniments, together with all the necessary apparatus were dispatched to Wales without delay, and within a week several records were secured. It was a great triumph for the company. Besides many of her favourite operatic airs, she placed upon the blanks such old English, Scottish, Irish and American tunes as " Coming through the Rye "; " Home, Sweet Home "; "Kathleen Mavourneen " ; " The Last Rose of Summer " ; " The Old Folks at Home " ; " Robin Adair " and " Within a mile o' Edinboro' Town." The vibrations of the sound waves of these were imbedded in the wax and carried off victoriously to London to be transferred to the disc composition in which they will remain until the crack of doom. Still, it is only right to, state that, as the company tell us in their illustrated catalogue, the art of recording the human voice has improved so rapidly since then that these records cannot with justice be compared with records of great artists which are now being issued. Nevertheless, they give a remarkably good idea of the richness and flexibility of Patti's notes.

The earliest recordings of Caruso were made as far back as 1902, shortly after the famous Neapolitan had set all Italy ablaze with the wonder of his singing. No sooner did the news of this epoch-moving phenomenon reach

England than the Gramophone Company determined to make a capture of his voice at all hazards. Emissaries were appointed to proceed to Milan, where the new tenor was then appearing at La Scala, and the journey was undertaken in hot haste. These ambassadors were furnished with a full equipment for recording the voice, and were empowered to make terms with the

By the courtesy of the   Gramophone Co., Ltd.

CARICATURE OF CARUSO MAKING A RECORD
Drawn by himself

great vocalist whatever they might be. It was an enterprise which must not be allowed to fail. They found Caruso a most amiable and genial young gentleman quite willing to accede to their proposals—for a consideration. That consideration was by no means a small one, but the emissaries having *carte blanche* everything was satisfactorily arranged, the tenor of tenors entered into an agreement to sing for no other recording company, and the agreement was most faithfully adhered to for twenty years. Caruso's notes can be heard on no other discs than those of " His Master's

Voice." During the whole of that long period he made no fewer than 112 solos for the company, besides taking part in 32 duets, 4 trios, 6 quartets, 1 quintet and 2 sextets, 157 records in all.

Dame Nellie Melba, the most gifted soprano of the later years of last century and, as far as they have gone, of this, has made a great many delightful records for the Gramophone Company. It has been complained by some

By the courtesy of the Gramophone Co., Ltd

DAME NELLIE MELBA

that, in technical phrase, she does not record well, which means, of course, that her voice is not reproduced with that faithful adherence to the original which is required. That, we believe, to be a defect which can be easily explained. The clear, liquid limpidity of Melba's notes does not create such a disturbance of sound waves as those of a more dramatic and impassioned singer. The consequence is that the vibrations are more evenly marked upon the wax, which gives the impression to the listener of a lack of force and character. Melba, perhaps, possesses the purest soprano of any woman who ever sang. It is absolutely faultless in its clarity, but by reason of her nature—she is of Scottish descent, though born near Melbourne, in Australia—it has not the excessive warmth and brilliancy of colour which belong to the voices of the daughters of the passionate lands bordering on the Mediterranean. Detached from the glamour which inevitably surrounds the stage Melba's notes sound a trifle cold, and hence to the ordinary person who listens to her records comes that slight feeling of disappointment.

There is not a musician or singer who has attained any celebrity whose voice or playing is not more familiar to the gramophone enthusiast of to-day than it is to the wealthiest music-lover in the world who is without a talking machine. The gramophone user can always have his records beside him to listen to when he is in the mood. We have only mentioned the names of a few of the great singers whose voices have been recorded, but we can safely say that there is not one living vocal artist of note whose musical tones have not been enshrined within a disc.

The Columbia Company have their own treasures in music. Dame Clara Butt is one of them, now recording only for Columbia. Stracciari, the great baritone, Barrientos, Stralia, Ponselle, the famous sopranos, are others. Among instrumentalists there are such honoured names as Pachmann and Busoni, pianists of the highest order, Ysaye, the veteran violinist, and Casals, indubitably the world's greatest 'cellist. Further, music lovers are indebted to Columbia for introducing chamber music, through the medium of the London String Quartet, on the gramophone.

But one of the greatest Columbia achievements is in connection with orchestral works. They persuaded

Sir Henry J. Wood to recant his previous objections to recording, and with his aid began to develop the interpretative side. Then followed Sir Thomas Beecham, Mr Albert Coates with the London Symphony Orchestra, .and Mr. Hamilton Harty with the Hallé Orchestra. These famous conductors have given us through Columbia new orchestral classics, including such works as " Scheherazade," " Le Chasseur Maudit " (The Accursed Hunter), Scriabin's " Poem of Ecstasy," " Siegfried Idyll," thus creating a new and higher standard in orchestral music alone. This, in itself, has gone far to secure recognition for the gramophone among scoffers and sceptics.

If we were to give a list of all the " stars of the record world," however, which scintillate for the various manufacturers, we would require more pages of our handbook than time and space can afford. It would be well, nevertheless, to draw attention to the fact that records have been made by others than musicians. We have spoken elsewhere of Mr. Gladstone having made a record. He was the first of statesmen to submit his voice to the tender mercies of the recording needle, but in the long ago such performances were not too successful. Of late years, however, with all the new inventions, both in recording and in reproduction, the speech of a minister can be listened to with quite as much attention as if it were delivered in a hall. Mr. Asquith, Earl Balfour and Mr. Lloyd George have each made records, and we rather think Mr. Winston Churchill may be added to the list. Elocutionary efforts by popular actors have also been a feature of the gramophone. The talking record, as it is called, is by no means a rarity. The late Sir H. Beerbohm Tree made a few, and we remember an exceptionally funny one by that clever entertainer, now dead, Snazelle   Bransby Williams has recorded most of his recitations and sketches, and there are many others.

Of actresses, as we think we have elsewhere mentioned, Sara Bernhardt has had her beautiful tones immortalized in shellac, but the ladies of the dramatic stage generally do not seem to take so kindly to the recording horn as their sisters of the lyric or operatic. The best that we have heard is a powerful recitation by Constance Collier, " The Hell-gate of Soissons " ; but what a glorious treat it would be if somebody could persuade Miss Ellen Terry, while she is still in possession of all the beauty of her remarkable speaking voice, to make a record of her wonderful delivery of Portia's speech in the " Merchant of Venice." Posterity would thank her for it.

The big manufacturing companies have given us the music of complete operas, so that a whole party can sit down in a drawing-room and listen to " Il Trovatore " or " Faust " or " Lohengrin " from beginning to end with as much pleasure as if they were seated in a stall at the opera. The Pathé Company has even done better than that, for it has recorded Molière's comedy of the " Malade Imaginaire " almost without a cut, and there is no reason why we should not have a Shakesperian play presented to us in the same way. At the present time the Gramophone Company are bringing out the whole series of Gilbert and Sullivan operas one by one, with fine casts. " The Mikado," " The Gondoliers," and " The Pirates of Penzance " have already been issued, and the others will follow in due course. The Columbia Company have sent their recording staff to Milan on separate occasions to secure complete performances of " Carmen," " Rigoletto " and " Aïda," as performed by the company of the famous La Scala Theatre. Such enterprises as these cost huge sums, but no amount is begrudged when an exact reproduction is to be obtained. Similarly, successful London musical plays are recorded by the original theatre artists for home enjoyment, and these have a great vogue.

Experiments have been made in getting the notes of singing birds, but these have not been altogether success-ful, because you cannot get a bird to sing to order. You may catch a portion of his song fitfully, but you cannot be sure of him. Some years ago there was a fuss made of a certain American, Professor Garner, who was to go out to Central Africa with recording apparatus, live in a cage in the tropical forest and record the language of apes. Whether the expedition was successful or not we cannot say. But, if the monkey tongue, supposing it should exist, has not been recorded, almost every spoken language on the face of the earth has. The recording expert travels far, and, though his baggage is not quite so light as that of the photographer, he has succeeded in making valuable additions to philological and ethnological science. In this direction there is a vast field still open for scientific inquiry, and if some of the learned societies could find the money to prosecute research in remote lands and among little known peoples, the results would be most interesting. By language we might be able to trace the origins of races.

The Japanese do quite an extensive trade with China by making Chinese records, and we believe Mr. Russell Hunting contrived to secure many excellent discs of the queer agglutinate tongue of the inhabitants of the Flowery Land during a brief sojourn there. The enterprising Japs are piercing into India, too, where they are making records of the various dialects, thereby casting a reflection upon our British industrial methods. There is wealth among the Hindus as well as poverty, and doubtless a considerable trade might be tapped by selling machines with native records.

There is not a musical instrument which has not been brought under subjection by the recorder. Of late the Hawaiian ukalele, a species of guitar, said to have been introduced to the islands of the Pacific by the early Spanish missionaries, and adapted by the natives to their own requirements in the way of music, has become quite a cult among gramophone users. It emits a peculiar plaintive sound by sliding the finger up and down the strings while the right hand twangs an accompaniment. Many of the best native performers have been in this country and made records, and the voices are strangely sweet. Several were engaged in a successful piece at the Prince of Wales's Theatre entitled " The Bird of Paradise," where their songs and playing attracted much attention.

Since the war dancing has become, one might say, our most popular pastime, and the talking machine provides a ready means for supplying the music. On this account there has been a huge output of dance records, the abominable jazz taking the lead for a long time. Thank goodness this nuisance is being somewhat abated. There were records made from bands and orchestras which played nothing but this hideous importation from America, and all of them were faithfully reproduced on discs. The poor reviewers of the trade organs were absolutely deafened by them.

Before closing this chapter on record makers, it may not be out of place to mention a record which was made by an army and all its guns. The late Mr. Gaisberg of the Gramophone Company was permitted by the military authorities to approach within the lines during the bombardment of Lille for the purpose of recording the din of war. The result, however, was rather disappointing.

CHAPTER IX

FROM the earliest days of talking machine manufacture and distribution in this country the friendly rivalry (a notable feature of most new industries) existing between the various houses engaged in the trade was not conducive to the formation of a Trade Association. At social and other gatherings of the industry it was talked of, but there appeared to be no urgent necessity for it in those days, so no definite action was taken. The common trials and tribulations of the war period, however, brought the talking machine manufacturers and traders more closely together and emphasized the need for concerted action.

The difficulties of the trade in the years of war were immense. For a considerable period the gramophone was regarded by a certain section of the Government as a luxury, and it required the most strenuous exertions on the part of some of the leaders in the business to prevent the industry being relegated into the sorely tried position of a "luxury trade." For a time all effort seemed hopeless and the trade appeared to be doomed. Just then, however, when things were darkest, energetic action was taken by the British Music Trades Industry Committee, an emergency war-time organization, in the formation and conduct of which prominent members of the talking machine industry took part, notably Mr. M. E. Ricketts (then of the Gramophone Co., Ltd.), who acted as Honorary Secretary throughout its existence and did yeoman service. As a result of this collective representation the trade was

94

undoubtedly saved and adequate supplies of materials assured.

When one looks back upon the active part that the gramophone played in bringing comfort and joy to the boys who were at the front, it is almost inconceivable that the Government should have adopted the attitude it did.   However, that is all past and gone, but we must rot forget the men who upheld the rights of the trade that supplied the music which encouraged our devoted lads.

It was apparent from the outset of the struggle to obtain recognition of the talking machine as a powerful, and indeed vital, force for the good of the nation and its preservers that the music trade was inefficiently organized, and the long talked of Association of Gramophone Manufacturers and Dealers took shape in the minds of the leaders of the industry.   In the negotiations between the British Music Trades Industry Committee and the Government on the question of supplies of material it was found that the musical instrument (small goods) makers had many interests in common with those of the talking machine trade.   Consequently in the early months of the year 1918 Mr. M. E. Ricketts, Mr. Frank Samuel (Barnett, Samuel & Sons, Ltd.) and Mr. Walter B. Beare (Beare & Son) all young, vigorous men in the trade, called together a historic meeting at the Midland Grand Hotel, St. Pancras (then the headquarters of music trade activities). Representatives of leading houses in the talking machine and musical instrument (small goods) trades were invited and all attended.   The proposed association met with spontaneous and unanimous approval, and the difficulty of securing a suitable and energetic organizer was overcome when Mr. Chas. E. Timms, also a young and active man with a life-long experience of the musical instrument trade, undertook the duties of Secretary.

In addition to those already named as promoters of the preliminary arrangements for the formation of the Association, there were several other gentlemen well known in the trade. Of these we may mention Mr. H. J. Cullum (Messrs. Lockwoods & Perophone, Ltd.) ; Mr M. F. Cooksey (J. Thibouville-Lamy & Co.) ; Mr. J. E. Hough (J E. Hough, Ltd.) ; Mr. W. Manson (The Gramophone Co., Ltd.) ; Mr. Geo. Murdoch (The Murdoch Trading Co.) ; Mr. A. J. Stavridi (Craies & Stavridi) ; Mr. Louis Sterling and Mr. J. Van Allen Shields (Columbia Graphophone Co., Ltd) ; Mr. Robert Willis (British Polyphon Co), and Mr. E. C. Paskell (Colmore Depot, Birmingham).

A draft constitution and rules were quickly evolved and approved ; an anticipated first season's membership of about fifty houses was, by energetic application, amplified into an actual original associate roll of 118 houses, and on Tuesday, 25th June, 1918, The Association of Gramophone and Musical Instrument Manufacturers and Wholesale Dealers became an accomplished fact. The somewhat unwieldy nomenclature came in for careful consideration and criticism, but it was finally decided that the wide interests of the society could not be covered under a more curtailed title. Of the founders of the Association, Mr. M. E. Ricketts was at the first general meeting unanimously elected as President, with Mr. Frank Samuel, Vice-President ; Mr. W. B. Beare, Hon. Treasurer, and Mr C. E. Timms, Secretary. The Council of the Association is comprehensive and embraces every branch of the industry. At date (1921) it comprises—

Mr. W. B. Beare (Beare & Son).
Mr. D J. Blaikley (Boosey & Co.).

Mr. M. F. Cooksey (J. Thibouville-Lamy & Co.).

Mr. H. J. Cullum, M.B E (Perophone, Ltd.).

Mr. Herbert W. Dawkins (Thos. Dawkins & Co., Ltd.).

Mr. Geoffrey Hawkes (Hawkes & Son).

Mr. J. E. Hough (J. E. Hough, Ltd.).

Mr. A. G. Houghton (Houghton & Sons, Birmingham).

Mr. W. Manson (The Gramophone Co., Ltd.)

Mr. A J. Mason (Aeolian Co., Ltd.).

Mr. Geo. Murdoch (Murdoch Trading Co.).

Mr. E. C. Paskell (Colmore Depot, Birmingham)

Mr. Frank Samuel (Barnett, Samuel & Sons, Ltd.).

Mr. Louis Sterling (Columbia Graphophone Co., Ltd.).

The Constitution of the Association provides that there shall be elected annually a President and a Vice-President (each alternately from the Gramophone and Musical Instrument Industries), a Treasurer and a Council which shall consist of the officers and eleven members of the Association, six representing the Gramophone Trade and five the Musical Instrument Trade. Provision is also made for the formation of sub-committees representing : (1) The manufacturers of gramophones and/or their accessories. (2) The manufacturers of gramophone records. (3) Gramophone wholesale dealers. (4) The manufacturers of musical instruments and/or their accessories. (5) Musical instrument wholesale dealers. To these would be added by consent of the Council other sub-committees should occasion arise.

Membership is open to any bona fide British company, firm or person engaged in the trades concerned and carrying on business within Great Britain and Ireland, subject to election by the Council.

The objects of the Association are : " To promote, protect and secure the varied interests of manufacturers of, and wholesale dealers in, Gramophones, Musical Instruments and their Accessories, and to use every endeavour to obtain fair conditions and whole-hearted support for British Manufacturers and Wholesale Dealers." That these aims have been adequately fulfilled during the first three years of the Association's existence is shown by a *résumé* of the more important questions dealt with by the Council in that period on behalf of the members. Taking a cursory glance through these we find prominently—

Safeguarding of supplies of materials in the post war period.

Propaganda calling the attention of the whole of the Music Trade of this country to the menace of the proposed Luxury Tax and action to avert same.

Employment of Disabled Soldiers and Sailors in the Industry.

Railway Rates and Conditions.

Import Duty.

Merchandise Marks Act.

Excess Profits Duty.

Organization of, and support for, the Federation of British Music Industries

Music Trades Joint Industrial Council.

British Music Industries' Scientific Research Association.

Fraudulent Advertising of Gramophones, etc.

Monthly Publication of Imports and Exports Statistics.

Customs Drawback on Re-exportation.

Imports from Germany.

Trade Conditions in Germany.

Music Trades School.

British Industries Fair.

British Music Convention.

Net Sales Certificates Trade Press.

The work of the Association is recorded in the trade Press and also in an " Association Newsletter " which is circulated to all members periodically.

It is agreeable to state that the success of the Association is attributable to the indefatigable zeal and attention of the clever Secretary, Mr. Chas. E. Timms, and it is certain that no Association or body of men banded together with a common object can be really successful unless there is one man with the driving power and the will and energy to devote to it.

No sooner had the manufacturers and wholesale traders set their Association going on a solid basis than the retail dealers began to think about organizing. For some time there had been formed in the provinces various District Associations, but there was no central combinations and these scattered organizations had no coherency. Before the new plant took root much spade work was accomplished by Mr. S. N. Shand, of Stratford, London, who spared no labour on the scheme he had taken in hand. In an unobtrusive fashion he was well backed up by Mr. Robert Poulter, the manager of *The Talking Machine News*, the oldest and best gramophone trade organ in the world, who had also lent an untiring hand in the formation of the Gramophone and Musical Instrument and Wholesale Dealers Association. Eventually the new idea took shape and a first meeting was called for 22nd September, 1920. The attendance was most encouraging. Officers were then and there elected, Mr. Rasin Jones, of Manchester, being appointed President for the first year, with Mr. E. Marshall as Vice-President. The members of Committee were Messrs. Gerald Forty, S. E. Moon,

8—(1466E)

C. J. Price, J. H. Riley and F. E. Stokes, while Mr. S. N. Shand was unanimously elected Hon. Secretary.

The first business, after the election of office-bearers, was to deal with the establishment of branches throughout the kingdom and the affiliation of existing organizations The members present were most enthusiastic, and resolved upon adopting a personal campaign in their several districts for the purpose of augmenting membership. The nominal subscription was fixed at 21s., to be sent to Mr. S. N. Shand, 150 The Grove, Stratford, London, E.15.

The Association being so young we have not sufficient data to go upon to record its progress, but we understand that it is already in a very flourishing condition, and that many matters of great importance to the retail trade are being investigated and will ultimately be decided upon.

The Federation of British Music Industries does not exactly come within our province to dilate upon, but it is well to observe that the gramophone industry is strongly represented therein, and that at all the conventions and meetings the talking machine interests are carefully looked after. With such a Chairman as Mr. Alexander Dow, whose knowledge and experience of every branch of the musical profession and trade is unequalled, the Federation has a man at its head of unique personality, embodying both culture and charm.[1] The work of the Federation is educational and propagandist, and every British musician of note has identified himself with its objects. It wields a powerful influence over musical art in many directions, and this influence is beginning to make itself manifest in the keener

[1] Since this was written Mr. Louis Sterling, of the Columbia Gramophone Company, has succeeded Mr. Dow for a year.   A big feather in the cap of the Talking Machine Industry.

interest which is being taken in music by the nation at large.

Some years ago it was felt by talking machine enthusiasts that the instrument was not sufficiently known and understood. Societies were, therefore, inaugurated with the intention of inducing the public to form a deeper estimation of the invention. At that time, it must be recollected, prejudice against what was derisively called " canned " music ran exceedingly high, and it was not altogether without reason, for some of the cheaper records and machines were atrociously bad (a few of them are so still, as anyone can find out for himself if he will take the trouble to walk through a poorer class neighbourhood of an evening). But these were not the instruments nor records which the societies were experimenting with. They were going in for better things and were wishful to demonstrate the finest that had been manufactured.

We are under the impression that the North London Gramophone and Phonograph Society was the first to be established, with that ardent and learned experimenter, Henry Seymour, as President. We may be wrong, but our researches have not given us an earlier one. The long-continued feud between cylinder and disc adherents is nowhere so rancorous as among the members of the societies. Edison is worshipped as a super-man by certain communities, while the followers of the needle-cut disc will have none of him. Of one thing, however, there can be little doubt, the gramophone people triumph over their opponents most mightily in the matter of artists. A gramophone society can put up a concert with all the picked voices of the world upon the programme, whereas the phonograph admirers have to be content with only those American performers who are not in the front rank of opera or platform. The phonograph supporters also labour under another disability. The whole of their records, cylinder or disc, have to come across from America, for they scorn every other make save that of the Great Panjandrum himself

Throughout the length and breadth of the land these societies are springing up, not only in the big towns, but in what our theatrical friends call " the smalls," and even in villages. The meetings are generally held once a month, when all the most recent issues from the record manufacturers are listened to and their merits discussed. New sound boxes, needles and other accessories are also tried over and pronounced upon. In short, the societies are composed of enthusiasts who allow nothing that is fresh to escape them. Many of the members are themselves inventors, who, by their connection with the societies, get their inventions tested. Whether this is an advantage or not is somewhat doubtful, for the doings are reported in the trade Press, and the publicity thus obtained may not always be for the benefit of the inventor. However, there can be no denying that the societies are doing a vast amount of good to the industry by their propaganda work, and we should be the very last to cavil at the spirit with which the members are imbued.

CHAPTER X

No less important authority than Sir Edward Elgar, O.M , has predicted for the gramophone a great future as an instructor of youth in music. We have already seen how it is thus employed in America, but we lag slowly behind. The ingrained conservatism of the Briton restrains him from advance. He hesitates and boggles at an innovation, whereas the more acute American grasps the situation and with far-seeing intelligence adapts it to his needs. The old and deeply rooted prejudice · against the talking machine still obtains in the official mind, and however strong may be the efforts of the more liberal spirits, the educational authorities in many directions block the way.

In spite of the opposition, however, there is a movement going on which may ultimately triumph over all obstacles and place our country on the same level that our friends across the Atlantic have gained. Canada has awakened to a sense of the educational advantages which can be reaped by a practical use of the talking machine as teacher, and is introducing it into many schools of the Dominion. The governing bodies there, being in closer proximity to the United States, have viewed with observant eyes the benefits derived from the employment of the gramophone as a training factor among the children, with the result that, unless we actively bestir ourselves, the motherland will find herself outstripped in musical knowledge by her own offspring. This is lamentable, but it is perfectly true, and we have nothing to blame but the obduracy of our officialdom.

Sir Edward Elgar has urged upon those having charge of the young, and Mr. Percy A Scholes has written in a booklet published by the Gramophone Company, addressed to teachers, the duty of instruction in that very important point, Learning to Listen. It is the title of Mr. Scholes's brochure, and in the introduction, Dr. John Adams, Professor of Education at the University of London, dwells upon the importance of music in any scheme of education. Appreciation is the first principle in the knowledge of music, and the talking machine is the only instrument through which appreciation can be instilled into the mind, for it is the only instrument that can play *all* music. In his preface Mr. Scholes quotes Dr. Eliot, of Harvard, to the effect that the true understanding of music is " one of the best means of developing the human child, of drawing out its latent powers, and cultivating the human spirit." Hitherto, according to Mr. Scholes, musical education has been limited to making the child acquainted with only such music as it can perform itself or as on rare occasions can be performed for it. The talking machine has changed all that.

The other day Sir Edward Elgar said that he looked forward to the time when no school would be deemed complete without its proper number of gramophones. Surely Sir Edward's dictum should have some weight with county councils, for, besides being our greatest living British composer, he has given much time and thought to the subject of education.

Among other things of much interest in the little book by Mr. Scholes are several programmes of music which can all be played to a class on a gramophone. There are parts of the country, too, where no concerts in the ordinary sense can be heard either by children or adults, and for such districts the various lists of the works of great composers which he gives are useful in showing how appreciation can gradually be acquired by the use of a good machine and high-class records.

It is this learning to appreciate the best of music, not mere technical ability to play a piano, a violin or any other manipulatory instrument, that cultivates the mind, and Sir Edward Elgar is quite in agreement with this. Of course, there must be work as well if the child is to become an instrumentalist, but such work will be much more easy if the basis has been laid by the talking machine. In a letter to Lord Northcliffe, Paderewski, the renowned pianist, wrote : ": Education by good music is essential to the mind development of children in every country, and I should like to see a gramophone and a good selection of ' His Master's Voice ' records in every school."

And now, having mentioned " His Master's Voice " in this connection, we must congratulate the Gramophone Company upon the very active steps the great firm is taking in promoting this form of musical education. The propaganda initiated by them, growing stronger every day, is bound to have a marked influence upon the community at large. By literature of an easily grasped character, by lectures, not too technical, and by the issue of a graduated series of records the company is fighting their way through all opposition. They have constructed a strong-built machine for use in schools, which is sold at the not too exorbitant price of £25, and they assist in every way the teachers who have to demonstrate to the little learners the truths and beauties of the art which is being unfolded to them.

Beyond the point of imparting a taste for good music it is impossible for the gramophone to go. It simply takes the place of the singer, the instrumentalist and the orchestra, but we must remember how few children are in a position to hear the best of these except through the talking machine. It is amazingly democratic. At a comparatively small cost the off-spring of the poor can obtain as much pleasure in music

OPEN

CLOSED

By the courtesy of the   Gramophone Co., Ltd.

" HIS MASTER'S VOICE " GRAMOPHONE FOR SCHOOLS

as the heirs and heiresses of the rich, but that pleasure can only come through a course of instruction, unless the child be abnormally gifted. In the old days opera was a sealed book to most of the people, because of the prices charged, and in consequence the masses never acquired a taste for it. A few of the old airs from " Maritana " or the " Bohemian Girl " was all that reached them through solo singers on the platform or by the medium of sheet music, from which it was painfully strummed by amateurs on cheap pianos. Those days have gone. The gramophone brings real music into the home, though we must confess that we have no sympathy with a good deal of it. Much stuff is placed upon records which cannot be classed as music in the strict sense, and many machines are sold to the unwary which do not deserve the name of gramophone. These remarks, however, do not apply to " His Master's Voice." All goods which bear the famous trade-mark may be indisputably relied upon for quality and value.

There was perhaps as much indignation felt by some of the " heads " at Eton when Mr. Basil Johnson, the principal music master, proposed the introduction of a gramophone as animated Jennie Geddes, the old Scotswoman, when she heard the organ in the kirk and threw her stool at the minister's head. But Mr. Johnson had his way and a talking machine was installed, thereby setting an example to all the other public schools of Great Britain. We understand that Winchester, Repton and Oundle have already followed in the footsteps of Eton, and it is not improbable that, before this little book is published, all the great schools of England, Scotland and Wales will be provided with instruments.

In Wales, as was to be expected from such a musical nation, the movement is making headway with gigantic strides. This is chiefly owing to the efforts of Dr. Walford Davies, than whom the gramophone has no more strenuous advocate. Few men are more honoured in the Principality, or out of it, than the organist of the Temple Church, who is now Professor of Music in the University of Wales and Director of Music in Welsh Schools. His views are that each of the 1,800 Welsh elementary schools should have its gramophone, and he is also organizing the formation of record libraries. Dr. Davies is an authority who commands respect, and his advice prompts instant consideration. In Wales the seeds of his utterances fall upon fruitful ground, for, like all Celts, the Cymric are essentially an intensely musical people and respond with enthusiasm to any suggestion of education in music. Of the four races which are comprised in the British Isles none is so advanced musically as the Welsh, and it is only natural that the propaganda of Dr Davies should meet with a favourable reception. Thus, when the Professor was entertained to luncheon by the Rotary Club of Swansea, he gave a short lecture-recital on the gramophone to the members. There were present fifty-five business men keenly interested in every word which fell from the Doctor's lips. As he concluded his lecture Dr. Davies asked those who recognized the educational value of the gramophone to write to him for lists of suitable records for home study. To his surprise and satisfaction the applicants numbered sixty-two, showing that the Professor's appeal in the good cause had spread beyond the confines of the Rotary Club.

The Gramophone Company are efficiently backing up Dr. Davies's efforts by providing school machines and special records, so that Wales, as heretofore, will continue to maintain a priority in music unless strong endeavours are made in other directions.

Many persons are constantly referring to what they call the " good old days." We know very well that in almost every respect they were extremely bad old days, but we cannot gainsay the fact that, say in the spacious days of Queen Elizabeth, the common people, appallingly ignorant though they might have been, were more light-hearted and joyous than we are to-day.   Their folk-songs, their glees and madrigals point to it, and these bring us at a single step to the folk dances.

All English musicians know the interest Mr. Cecil Sharp takes in these matters.   He has travelled the country round picking up odd snatches of ancient ditties in out of the way nooks and corners of the land ; he has made friends with strange, eccentric village characters to get hold of a few bars of some old tune which they alone knew, and he has witnessed queer jigs and reels in places where the same dances were in vogue 500 years ago.   It is the darling wish of his heart to see those old dances re-introduced through the school-children of our time.   And why not ?   They were a thousand-fold more innocent than the tangos and fox-trots and bunny-hugs which have been brought here from the dancing saloons of the New York Bowery. The music to which our forefathers and foremothers footed it so bravely was infinitely preferable to the discordant abominations of jazz.   The old " contra " dances, perverted into " country," of which the " Hay-makers," the original of Sir Roger de Coverley, is a fine ensample, gave health and joy to the lads and lasses— a joy that is not experienced in the stifling ball-rooms of the town.   Why, then, should not Mr. Sharp's wish be fulfilled ?   Many of the old tunes, arranged by him, have been recorded and published, and with efficient teachers we could have our children instructed in them to the benefit of their health and morals.

We have spoken elsewhere of the teaching of languages by means of the gramophone, and we understand that this system is going ahead with considerable force.   Messrs. Pathé Frères issue many discs made from the speaking voices of the best enunciators in

French, Spanish and other European tongues. By this method a correct accent can be imparted to the pupils without the intervention of a master or mistress. The lessons, we believe, are graduated from the simplest sentences until they reach the conversational stage. Other companies, too, produce records of the same character, and Messrs. Funk and Wagnall, the educational publishers, have an American machine and records adapted to this system of instruction.

The amplification of sound for the purpose of filling large halls or for outdoor uses has engaged the attention of many inventors. There is the Naturafone, an excellent machine, the invention of our good friend Mr. Crowe, a son of the late Gwyllym Crowe, the waltz composer and conductor, several years ago, of the promenade concerts at Covent Garden. This instrument depends upon the construction of the sound box for its increase of volume. Then there is the Stentorphone, a huge machine, in which compressed air is forced through the tone-arm. Both these, however, are completely cast in the shade by the Magnavox or Telemegaphone, an electric contrivance from America which has just found its way to this country. This can be used either with a gramophone, or simply by a public speaker talking into a mouthpiece like that of a telephone. The sound can be regulated by the turning of a switch, and so great is its power that the human voice in certain conditions of the atmosphere has been heard at a distance of seven miles. It was much in evidence during the last presidential election in the States, and it ought to be useful for candidates at the next general election in the United Kingdom. The agents here are the Johnson Talking Machine Company, of Tottenham Court Road.

As we began by saying that the Talking Machine is

only in its infancy, so we conclude. There are vast possibilities for it as yet undiscovered, and when all avenues have been explored it may happen that the instrument will be found useful to man in ways as yet undreamt of.

APPENDIX

AFTER due consideration, we have come to the conclusion that the industry is at last bestirring itself. It has had rather a protracted period of somnolence from which it has only now begun to awaken. Since the body of this little work was written, changes have taken place in many respects which show that the infant is progressing more rapidly than in the past. Further discoveries in the properties of sound have been exercising with striking results the brains of scientists. Revolutionary inventions have been making their appearance, which in all probability will necessitate great alterations in the construction and look of the talking machine.

Foremost among the latter will be found to-day the novel contrivances of Mr. Pemberton Billing. This singularly ingenious gentleman has been experimenting for a long time upon improvements in the gramophone and has taken out several patents For the exploitation of these, a company has been formed under the designation of the " World Record, Limited," with an extensive and well-equipped factory at Chiswick.

The new record comprises many startling changes in the character of the disc, although the general appearance remains the same. By a controlling device which may be attached to any machine, the record plays several songs, instrumental solos, or orchestral selections, as the case may be, on one side. This economizes space, and naturally the reproduction lasts much longer in performance than with ordinary records. The first issue of these compendious discs was only placed upon the market in October last (1922), so that there has not yet been sufficient time to judge of their reception by the public ; however, the sales already have proved abnormally large, and there is every sign that the new record has justified its existence.

Ingenious as Mr. Pemberton Billing has shown himself to be in his invention of the multiple record, he has by no means exhausted all his powers upon it. The ." Trinity " gramophone is another novelty of his which the " World Record, Ltd.," has sprung upon us. As its name implies, it is actually three in one. In the first place, you see before you a solid-looking, well-polished concert-grand, with closed sound-doors. When a record is put on the turntable and the sound-doors opened, you listen as you would to any other gramophone ; but this is not all. After some slight manipulation of the winding-handle and tone-arm, a full-bodied table-grand is withdrawn and, if wanted, can be carried into another room or out into the garden. There is still, however, the third and last transformation to take place. This is accomplished by taking a useful drawer away from the original concert-grand and fitting it on the top of the table-grand by means of certain clips for the purpose. It now becomes the " Picnic Portable," with a strong leather handle for carrying it about. The " Trinity " is certainly a marvel of ingenuity, and extraordinarily cheap at nineteen guineas.

A third novelty marketed by the " World Record, Ltd.," is the " Vistavox." The great feature about this is the peculiarity of the sound-box and tone-arm, which can hardly be explained without an illustration. It has, however, special tonal qualities to recommend it, and thus, we believe, a future is ensured for it.

The C. H. Roberts Manufacturing Co., Ltd., of Camden Road, London, is a flourishing concern which has recently placed several valuable machines upon the market under the style and title of " Bestone." Their first venture was the " Bestone " Portable, which was the invention of Mr. C. H. Roberts, a gentleman who for years has been a keen gramophone enthusiast and inventor of many original devices. The " Bestone " Portable is a gramophone, the interior framework of which is made of aluminium, a metal which not only has excellent acoustic advantages, but is also impervious to climatic changes.   Thus the model is as admirably adapted to the tropics as it is to frigid regions.

The Roberts Company have also just brought out the " Bestone " Corner Cabinet, a gramophone which fits into a corner, and is incomparable in tone and quality. It is a beautiful specimen of the cabinet-maker's art, and may be had in oak, mahogany, or lacquer at prices ranging from thirty-five to sixty-five guineas.   The company have at the same time issued a sound-box of superior make and finish at a guinea each.

A great novelty from the same firm is the Boys' Gramophone Outfit, which enables a boy to build up his own table cabinet and, after playing, pull it to pieces again, no glue or tacks being required in the process.   For ingenious youngsters this is a most enticing commodity.

When a big corporation like the Chappell Piano Co., Ltd , which is known and esteemed throughout the whole world, become sole sales concessionaires for a new invention, it is a sure guarantee of its excellence. This is what has happened in the case of the Cliftophone.   The inventor of this very fine machine is a gentleman named Clifton, of great scientific attainments, who has devoted many years to the study of sound reproduction.   After much labour, he has evolved a gramophone which may be looked upon as the very last word in talking machines.   As might be expected from the work which has been bestowed upon·it, the Cliftophone exhibits certain valuable improvements. These have been achieved by means of alterations in the accessories rather than through changes in the actual machine. The sound-box is of a novel construction, being fitted with a compensating lever as the connection between the diaphragm and the stylus-bar, thus dispensing with that tendency to work loose and give a disagreeable rattle, which is the fault of some of the ordinary sound-boxes. In the Cliftophone sound-box there is absolutely no possibility of this loosening. Again, the " Twin Reed " composite diaphragm is an innovation which emerges triumphantly from all tests. It has been the result of countless experiments and, as a consequence, has reached the highest pinnacle of perfection in regard to the properties of diaphragms.

Another remarkable feature of the Cliftophone is the tone-arm, with its continuation, the reproducing chamber. In this it has been the object of the inventor to make the reproduction truly realistic, and to that end he has introduced a special " articulation " or hinge for the tone-arm, which entirely prevents any " shake " or loss of motion, yet compels it to offer absolutely rigid resistance to the " drag " of the needle Thus the whole of the music may be heard without the slightest loss. The tone chambers, too, have been so designed as to secure the melodious and rhythmical development of the music emitted by the sound-box until it reaches the ear of the listener.

From unsolicited testimonials it would appear that the Cliftophone has succeeded in overcoming the prejudices of hardened gramophone haters and in drawing forth the admiration of the most scientific sound specialists.

As was said of old concerning books, so might it be repeated now with regard to sound-boxes : " Of the making of boxes there is no end." Why there should be this plethora of resonators is beyond our explanation, but to us it would seem as if every amateur artificer who had conceived some spite against the gramophone had forthwith started out to vent his spleen upon the instrument. The result of such inexpert efforts is the production of an accessory calculated to give the most acute tortures to the listener. A bad sound-box is worse than gout or toothache. It jars upon the auditory nerves and produces agony.

That the Talking Machine Industry is making much more rapid strides in advancement than has been observable for several years is a fact which not even the most prejudiced of its detractors can deny. It has overcome all unreasonable prepossessions and antiquated conservative bias by the soundness of its propositions and the strictly scientific principles upon which they have been carried out.

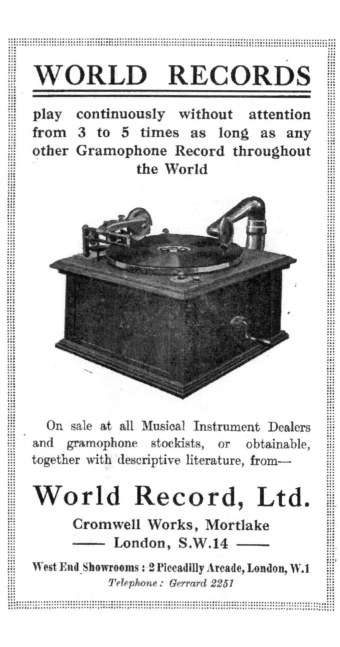

INDEX

118

Printed in Bath, England, by Sir Isaac Pitman & Sons, Ltd.
x—(1466E)

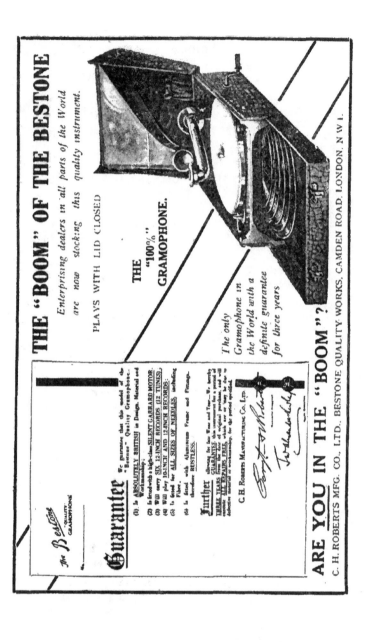

ARITHMETIC

PRICE

Arithmetic and Book-keeping.
By THOS. BROWN, F.S.S., and VINCENT E. COLLINGE,
A.C.I.S. In two parts.
Part I . . . . Net 2/6
Part II . . . . Net 1/3

Arithmetic of Commerce.
By P. W. NORRIS, M.A., B.Sc. (Hons.) . . Net 4/–

Complete Commercial Arithmetic. 3/–
Answers . . . . Net 1/6

Complete Mercantile Arithmetic.
With Elementary Mensuration.
By H. P. GREEN, F.C.Sp.T. (With Key) . Net 6/–

Arithmetic—contd.

BOOK-KEEPING AND ACCOUNTANCY

Bookkeeping and Accountancy—contd.

3

Bookkeeping and Accountancy—contd.

PRICE

Dictionary of Book-keeping.
By R. J. PORTERS . . . . . . Net 7/6

Elements of Book-keeping.
By W. O. BUXTON, A.C.A. (Hons.) . . . Net 2/6

Full Course in Book-keeping.
By H. W. PORRITT and W. NICKLIN, A.S.A.A. Net 5/-

Higher Book-keeping and Accounts.
By H. W. PORRITT and W. NICKLIN, A.S.A.A. Net 5/-

Hotel Book-keeping. Net 2/6

How to Become a Qualified Accountant.
By R. A. WITTY, A.S.A.A. . . . . Net 3/6

Manual of Book-keeping and Accounting.
By A. NIXON, F.C.A., and H. E. EVANS, A.C.A. . Net 10/6

Manual of Cost Accounts.
By H. JULIUS LUNT . . . . . Net 7/6

Manufacturing Book-keeping and Costs.
By G. JOHNSON, F.C.I.S. . . . . Net 5/-

Municipal Book-keeping.
By J. H. McCALL . . . . . . Net 7/6

Notes of Lessons on Book-keeping.
By J. ROUTLEY . . . . . . Net 3/6

Practical Book-keeping.
By G. JOHNSON, F.C.I.S. . . . . Net 6/-

Principles of Auditing.
By F. R. M. DE PAULA, O.B.E., F.C.A. . . Net 7/6

Primer of Book-keeping. 2/-

Principles of Book-keeping Explained.
By I. H. HUMPHRYS . . . . . Net 2/6

Questions and Answers in Book-keeping and Accounting.
By F. F. SHARLES, F.S.A.A., A.C.I.S. . . Net 10/6

Railway Accounts and Finance.
By ALLEN E. NEWHOOK, A.K.C. . . . Net 5/-

Shopkeepers' Accounts Simplified.
By C. D. CORNELL . . . . . Net 2/-

Sinking Funds, Reserve Funds, and Depreciation.
By J. H. BURTON, A.S.A.A. . . . . Net 3/6

Theory and Practice of Costing.
By E. W. NEWMAN, A.C.A. . . . . Net 10/6

4

BUSINESS TRAINING, COPY BOOKS, ETC.

		PRICE
Business Handwriting.	Net	1/6
Business Methods and Secretarial Work for Girls and Women. By HELEN REYNARD, M.A. . . . . . Net		2/6
Commercial Handwriting and Correspondence.	Net	2/6
Commercial Practice. By ALFRED SCHOFIELD . . . . . . Net		4/–
Counting-House Routine. 1st Year's Course. By VINCENT E. COLLINGE, A.C.I.S. . . . Net		1/9
Counting-House Routine. 2nd Year's Course. By VINCENT E. COLLINGE, A.C.I.S. . . . Net		3/6
Course in Business Training. By G. K. BUCKNALL, A.C.I.S.		2/6
Elements of Commerce. By F. HEYWOOD, A.C.I.S. . . . . Net		4/–
Handbook for Commercial Teachers. By FRED HALL, M.A., B.Com., F.C.I.S. . . Net		2/6
How to Become a Private Secretary. By J. E. McLACHLAN, F.I.P.S. . . . Net		3/6
How to Enter the Mercantile Marine. By R. A. FLETCHER . . . . . Net		3/6
How to Teach Business Training. By F. HEELIS, F.C.I.S. . . . . . Net		2/6
How to Write a Good Hand. By B. T. B. HOLLINGS . . . . . Net		1/6
Junior Woman Secretary. By ANNIE E. DAVIS, F.Inc.S.T. . . . Net		2/–
Manual of Business Training.	Net	5/–
Modern Business and Its Methods. By W. CAMPBELL, Chartered Secretary. . . Net		7/6
Office Routine for Boys and Girls. In three stages. First Stage		8d.
Second and Third Stages . . . . Each		1/–
Popular Guide to Journalism. By A. KINGSTON . . . . . . Net		2/6

Business Training, Copy Books, etc.—contd.

PRICE

Practical Journalism and Newspaper Law.
By A. BAKER, M.J.I., and E. A. COPE . . Net **3/6**

Principles and Practice of Commerce.
By JAMES STEPHENSON, M.A., M.Com., B.Sc. . Net **8/6**

Principles of Business.
By JAMES STEPHENSON, M.A., M.Com., B.Sc.
Part I . . . . Net **3/–**
Part II . . . . Net **3/6**

Routine of Commerce.
By ALFRED SCHOFIELD . . . . . Net **4/–**

Theory and Practice of Commerce.
Being a Complete Guide to Methods and Machinery of Business.
Edited by F. HEELIS, F.C.I.S. Assisted by Specialist Contributors . . . . Net **7/6**

CIVIL SERVICE

Civil Service Arithmetic Tests.
By P. J. VARLEY-TIPTON . . . . Net **2/6**

Civil Service Essay Writing.
By W. J. ADDIS, M.A. . . . . . Net **2/6**

Civil Service Guide.
By A. J. LAWFORD JONES . . . . Net **2/6**

Civil Service Practice in Précis Writing.
Edited by ARTHUR REYNOLDS, M.A. (Oxon) . Net **3/6**

Civil Servant and His Profession, The Net **3/6**

Copying Manuscript, Orthography, Handwriting, Etc.
By A. J. LAWFORD JONES. Actual Examination Papers only . . . . Net **3/6**

Digesting Returns into Summaries.
By A. J. LAWFORD JONES . . . . Net **2/6**

Elementary Précis Writing.
By WALTER SHAWCROSS, B.A. . . . Net **2/–**

Indexing and Précis Writing.
By A. J. LAWFORD JONES . . . . Net **2/6**

ENGLISH AND COMMERCIAL
CORRESPONDENCE

COMMERCIAL GEOGRAPHY AND
HISTORY

ECONOMICS

Economics—contd.

BANKING AND FINANCE

9

2

Banking and Finance—contd.

INSURANCE

PRICE

Actuarial Science, The Elements of.
By R. E. UNDERWOOD, M.B.E., F.I.A. . . Net 5/–

Common Hazards of Fire Insurance.
By W. G. KUBLER RIDLEY, F.C.I.I. . . Net 5/–

Guide to Life Assurance.
By S. G. LEIGH, F.I.A. . . . . . Net 5/–

Guide to Marine Insurance.
By HENRY KEATE . . . . . Net 3/6

Insurance.
By T. E. YOUNG, B.A., F.R.A.S., W. R. STRONG, F.I.A.,
and VYVYAN MARR, F.F.A., F.I.A. . . . Net 10/6

Insurance Office Organization, Management, and Accounts.
By T. E. YOUNG, B.A., F.R.A.S., and RICHARD
MASTERS, A.C.A. . . . . . . Net 6/–

Law and Practice as to Fidelity Guarantees.
By C. EVANS and F. H. JONES . . . Net 6/–

Motor Insurance.
By W. F. TODD . . . . . . Net 6/–

Pension, Endowment, Life Assurance, and Other Schemes for Commercial Companies.
By H. DOUGHARTY, F.C.I.S. . . . . Net 6/–

Principles of Insurance.
By J. ALFRED EKE . . . . . Net 3/6

Principles of Marine Law. (See page 19.)

Successful Insurance Agent, The.
By J. J. BISGOOD, B.A., F.C.I.S., J.P. . . Net 2/6

Talks on Insurance Law.
By J. A. WATSON, B.Sc., LL.B. . . . Net 5/–

Workmen's Compensation Insurance.
By C. E. GOLDING, LL.B., F.C.I.I. . . . Net 5/–

SHIPPING

Case and Freight Costs.
By A. W. E. CROSFIELD . . . . Net 2/–

Consular Requirements for Exporters and Shippers to all Parts of the World.
By J. S. NOWERY . . . . . . Net 7/6

Shipping—contd.

SECRETARIAL WORK

Secretarial Work—contd.

PRICE

Guide for the Company Secretary.
By ARTHUR COLES, F.C.I.S. . . . . Net 6/–

Guide to Company Secretarial Work.
By O. OLDHAM, A.C.I.S. . . . . Net 3/6

How to Become a Company Secretary.
By E. J. HAMMOND, A.C.I.S. . . . . Net 3/6

How to Become a Private Secretary.
By J. E. McLACHLAN . . . . . Net 3/6

How to Take Minutes.
Edited by E. MARTIN, F.C.I.S. . . . Net 2/6

Outlines of Transfer Procedure in Connection with Stocks, Shares, and Debentures of Joint Stock Companies.
By F. D. HEAD, B.A. (Oxon.), of Lincoln's Inn,
Barrister-at-Law . . . . . . Net 3/6

Practical Share Transfer Work.
By F. W. LIDDINGTON . . . . . Net 3/6

Prospectuses : How to Read and Understand Them.
By PHILIP TOVEY, F.C.I.S. . . . . Net 5/–

Questions and Answers on Secretarial Practice.
By E. J. HAMMOND, A.C.I.S. . . . . Net 7/6

Secretary's Handbook.
Edited by H. E. BLAIN, C.B.E. . . . Net 6/–

Transfer of Stocks, Shares, and Other Marketable Securities.
By F. D. HEAD, B.A. . . . . . Net 10/6

What is the Value of a Share ?
By D. W. ROSSITER . . . . Net 2/6

INCOME TAX

Corporation Profits Tax.
By P. D. LEAKE . . . . . . Net 1/–

Income Tax and Super Tax Practice.
By W. E. SNELLING . . . . . Net 12/6

Income Tax—contd.

PRICE

Practical Income Tax.
By W. E. SNELLING . . . . . Net 3/6

Super Tax Tables.
By G. O. PARSONS . . . . . . Net 1/-

Taxation Annual.
By W. E. SNELLING . . . . . Net 10/6

INDUSTRIAL ADMINISTRATION

Common Sense and Labour.
By S. CROWTHER . . . . . . Net 8/6

Current Social and Industrial Forces.
Edited by L. D. EDIE . . . . . Net 12/6

Employment Management.
Compiled and Edited by DANIEL BLOOMFIELD . Net 8/6

Factory Administration in Practice.
By W. J. HISCOX . . . . . . Net 8/6

Industrial Control (Applied to Manufacture).
By F. M. LAWSON, A.M.I.C.E., A.M.I.Mech.E. . Net 8/6

Lectures on Industrial Administration.
Edited by B. MUSCIO, M.A. . . . . Net 6/-

Management.
By J. LEE . . . . Net 5/-

Modern Industrial Movements.
Edited by D. BLOOMFIELD . . . . Net 10/6

Outlines of Industrial Administration.
By R. O. HERFORD, H. T. HILDAGE, and H. G. JENKINS
Net 6/-

Patents for Inventions.
By J. EWART WALKER, B.A., and R. BRUCE FOSTER, B.Sc.
Net 21/-

Principles of Industrial Administration, An Introduction to.
By A. P. M. FLEMING, C.B.E., M.Sc., M.I.E.E., and
H. J. BROCKLEHURST, M.Eng., A.M.I.E.E. . Net 3/6

Problems of Labour.
Compiled and Edited by DANIEL BLOOMFIELD . Net 8/6

Psychology of Management, The.
By L. M. GILBRETH . . . . . Net 7/6

14

Industrial Administration—contd.

15

Business Organization and Management— contd.

ADVERTISING AND SALESMANSHIP

16

Advertising and Salesmanship—contd.

BUSINESS HANDBOOKS AND WORKS

OF REFERENCE

17

Business Handbooks and Works of Reference–contd.

18

Law—contd.

Commercial Law of England, The.
By J. A. SLATER, B.A., LL.B. (Lond.) . . . Net 3/6

Companies and Company Law.
By A. C. CONNELL, LL.B. (Lond.) . . . Net 6/-

Company Case Law.
By F. D. HEAD, B.A. (Oxon) . . . Net 7/6

Elements of Commercial Law, The.
By A. H. DOUGLAS, LL.B. (Lond.) . . . Net 2/6

Elementary Law.
By E. A. COPE . . . . Net 5/-

Examination Notes on Commercial Law.
By R. W. HOLLAND, O.B.E., M.A., M.Sc., LL.D. Net 2/6

Examination Notes on Company Law.
By R. W. HOLLAND, O.B.E., M.A., M.Sc., LL.D. Net 2/6

Guide to Company Law.
By R. W. HOLLAND, O.B.E., M.A., M.Sc., LL.D. Net 3/6

Guide to Railway Law.
By ARTHUR E. CHAPMAN, M.A., LL.D. (Camb.) Net 7/6

Guide to Bankruptcy Law and Winding-up of Companies.
By F. PORTER FAUSSET, B.A., LL.B., *Barrister-at-Law* Net 3/6

Guide to the Law of Licensing.
By J. WELLS THATCHER . . . . Net 5/-

Inhabited House Duty.
By W. E. SNELLING . . . . . Net 12/6

Law of Contract, The.
By R. W. HOLLAND, M.A., M.Sc., LL.D., *of the Middle Temple, Barrister-at-Law* . . . . . Net 5/-

Law of Repairs and Dilapidations.
By T. CATO WORSFOLD, M.A., LL.D. . . Net 3/6

Law Relating to Secret Commissions and Bribes (Christmas Boxes, Gratuities, Tips, Etc.), The.
By ALBERT CREW, *Barrister-at-Law*. With American Notes by MORTEN Q. MACDONALD, LL.B. . Net 10/6

Law Relating to the Carriage by Land of Passengers, Animals, and Goods, The.
By S. W. CLARKE, *of the Middle Temple, Barrister-at-Law* . . . . Net ·7/6

19

Law—contd.

Law Relating to the Child : Its Protection, Education, and Employment, The.
By R. W. HOLLAND, O.B.E., M.A., M.Sc., LL.D.   Net   5/-

Law Relating to Trade Customs, Marks, Secrets, Restraints, Agencies, Etc., Etc., The.
By LAWRENCE DUCKWORTH, *Barrister-at-Law* . Net   1/3

Legal Aspect of Commerce, The.
By A. SCHOLFIELD, M.Com., A.C.I.S.   .   . Net   7/6

Legal Terms, Phrases, and Abbreviations.
By E. A. COPE   .   .   .   .   .   . Net   3/-

Mercantile Law.
By J. A. SLATER, B.A., LL.B. (Lond.)   .   . Net   7/6

Outlines of Company Law.
By F. D. HEAD, B.A. (Oxon.)   .   .   . Net   2/6

Partnership Law and Accounts.
By R. W. HOLLAND, O.B.E., M.A., M.Sc., LL.D.   Net   6/-

Principles of Marine Law.
By LAWRENCE DUCKWORTH   .   .   .   . Net   10/6

Questions and Answers in Commercial Law.
By R. W. HOLLAND   .   .   .   .   . Net   5/-

Railway (Rebates) Case Law.
By GEO. B. LISSENDEN .   .   .   .   . Net   10/6

Solicitor's Clerk's Guide.
By E. A. COPE   .   .   .   .   .   . Net   4/-

Wills, Executors and Trustees.
By J. A. SLATER, B.A., LL.B. (Lond.)   .   . Net   2/6

TRANSPORT

Industrial Traffic Management.
By G. B. LISSENDEN   .   .   .   .   . Net   21/-

History and Economics of Transport, The.
By A. W. KIRKALDY, M.A., B.Litt., M.Com., and
A. D. EVANS   .   .   .   .   .   . Net   15/-

How to Send Goods by Road, Rail, and Sea.
By G. B. LISSENDEN   .   .   .   .   . Net   2/-

Motor Road Transport for Commercial Purposes.
By J. PHILLIMORE   .   .   .   .   . Net   12/6

20

Digitized by Microsoft ®

PITMAN'S
COMMON COMMODITIES AND INDUSTRIES
SERIES

IN each volume of this series a particular product or industry is treated by an expert writer and practical man of business in an interesting non-technical style. Beginning with the life history of the plant, or other natural product, he follows its development until it becomes a commercial commodity, and so on through the various phases of its sale in the market and its purchase by the consumer. Industries are treated in a similar manner, so that these books form ideal introductions to the particular industries with which they deal.

In crown 8vo, about 150 pp., including many illustrations, and, where necessary, a map and diagrams. **3s.** net.

Tea.
By A. IBBETSON.
Coffee.
By B. B. KEABLE.
Sugar.
By GEO. MARTINEAU, C.B.
Oils.
By C. AINSWORTH MITCHELL.
Wheat and Its Products.
By ANDREW MILLAR.
Rubber.
By C. BEADLE and H. P. STEVENS, M.A., Ph.D., F.I.C.
Iron and Steel.
By C. HOOD.
Copper.
By H. K. PICARD.
Coal.
By FRANCIS H. WILSON, M.Inst.M.E.
Timber.
By W. BULLOCK.
Cotton.
By R. J. PEAKE.
Silk.
By LUTHER HOOPER.
Wool.
By J. A. HUNTER.
Linen.
By ALFRED S. MOORE.
Tobacco.
By A. E. TANNER.

Leather.
By K. J. ADCOCK.
Clays and Clay Products.
By ALFRED B. SEARLE.
Paper.
By HARRY A. MADDOX.
Soap.
By WILLIAM H. SIMMONS, B.Sc. (Lond.), F.C.S.
Glass and Glass Making.
By P. MARSON.
Gums and Resins.
By ERNEST J. PARRY, B.Sc., F.I.C., F.C.S.
The Boot and Shoe Industry.
By J. S. HARDING.
The Motor Industry.
By HORACE WYATT, B.A.
Gas and Gas Making.
By W. H. Y. WEBBER, C.E.
Furniture.
By H. E. BINSTEAD.
Coal Tar.
By A. R. WARNES, F.C.S., A.I.Mech.E.
Petroleum.
By A. LIDGETT.
Salt.
By A. F. CALVERT, F.C.S.
Zinc and Its Alloys.
By T. E. LONES, M.A., LL.D., B.Sc.

Common Commodities Series—Contd.

FOREIGN LANGUAGES

FRENCH

23

PORTUGUESE

PITMAN'S SHORTHAND

Pitman's Shorthand holds the world's record for speed and accuracy

For Complete List of Text-books, Phrase Books, Dictation Books, Reading Books, etc., see Pitman's " SHORTHAND AND TYPEWRITING CATALOGUE."

TYPEWRITING

Complete List post free on application.

Sir Isaac Pitman & Sons, Ltd., Parker St., Kingsway, London, W.C.2

Printed in Bath, England, by Sir Isaac Pitman & Sons, Ltd.
(2281w)

CPSIA information can be obtained
at www.ICGtesting.com
Printed in the USA
LVHW062234030822
725063LV00023BA/508

9 781376 205831